SUTTON POCKET HISTORIES

THE
CRUSADES

BERNARD HAMILTON

SUTTON PUBLISHING

First published in the United Kingdom in 1998 by
Sutton Publishing Limited · Phoenix Mill
Thrupp · Stroud · Gloucestershire · GL5 2BU

British Library Cataloguing in Publication Data
A catalogue record for this book is available from the British
Library.

ISBN 0-7509-1914-0

Cover illustration: Departure for the Crusades *(Bibliotheque
Nationale, Paris/ Bridgeman Art Library).*

ALAN SUTTON™ and SUTTON™ are the
trade marks of Sutton Publishing Limited

Typeset in 11/14.5 pt Baskerville.
Typesetting and origination by
Sutton Publishing Limited.
Printed in Great Britain by
The Guernsey Press Company Limited,
Guernsey, Channel Islands.

To Jan,
Sarah and Alice

Contents

Acknowledgements

I should like to thank the many undergraduates who have taken my courses on the crusades over the years, and also the members of the Adult Education classes I have taught on this subject, all of whom have helped me to a better understanding of the crusades. I also want to thank my wife who has good humouredly shared her marriage with the crusade movement.

Note: The translation of the Clermont decree on p. 2 is from L. and J. Riley-Smith, *The Crusades: Idea and Reality, 1095–1274* (London, Edward Arnold, 1981), p. 37.

List of Dates

1143	**8 April**. John II dies, is succeeded by Manuel I.
1144	**24 December**. Zengi captures Edessa.
1147	Lisbon captured with the help of an English fleet on its way to the Holy Land.
	German crusade against the Wends.
1148	Second Crusade unsuccessfully attacks Damascus.
1149	Nur ad-Din invades Antioch, Prince Raymond is killed.
1154	Nur ad-Din becomes ruler of Damascus.
1159	Emperor Manuel comes to Antioch and takes the Crusader States under his protection.
1163–9	Struggle for Egypt between Nur ad-Din and King Amalric of Jerusalem.
1169	Saladin becomes master of Egypt.
1171	**13 September**. End of the Fatimid Caliphate of Cairo.
1174	**15 May**. Death of Nur ad-Din.
	11 July. Death of King Amalric; Baldwin IV, the Leper, becomes King of Jerusalem.
	28 October. Saladin gains control of Damascus.
1177	**25 November**. Saladin is defeated at Montgisard by Baldwin IV and Reynald of Châtillon.
1186	Saladin completes his annexation of the Zengid lands.
1187	**4 July**. Saladin defeats Guy of Lusignan and the army of Jerusalem at the Battle of Hattin.
1189	August. Guy of Lusignan besieges Acre.
1190	**10 June**. Emperor Frederick I Barbarossa drowned in Cilicia while on crusade.

1191	**May**. Richard I annexes Cyprus.
	12 July. Acre surrenders to the Third Crusade.
	6 September. Richard I defeats Saladin at the Battle of Arsuf.
1192	**2 September**. Richard and Saladin make peace.
1193	**4 March**. Death of Saladin.
1197	**28 September**. The death of the Emperor Henry VI brings his crusade to an end.
1199–1229	Bishop Albert of Riga organizes the conquest of Livonia.
1204	**April**. Fourth Crusade sacks Constantinople and sets up the Latin Empire there.
1209–29	Albigensian Crusade is fought (with some intervals).
1212	Children's Crusade.
	16 July. Peter II of Aragon defeats the Moors at Las Navas de Tolosa.
1215	**November**. Fourth Lateran Council meets in Rome.
1218–21	Fifth Crusade attacks Egypt.
1225	**9 November**. The Emperor Frederick II marries Isabel II of Jerusalem.
1226	By the Golden Bull of Rimini Frederick II grants the Teutonic Order sovereignty over its conquests in Prussia.
1229	**18 February**. Treaty of Jaffa between Frederick II and al-Kamil: Jerusalem is restored to Christian rule.
1229–66	The Great Reconquest. All the Iberian peninsula

	except Granada is brought under direct Christian rule.
1230–95	Conquest of Prussia by the Teutonic Knights.
1231–36	Civil war in the Kingdom of Jerusalem between Frederick II's supporters and those of John of Ibelin.
1237–42	Attack by the Mongol horde on Russia and Eastern Europe.
1239–41	Theobald of Navarre and Richard of Cornwall negotiate the restoration of much territory to the Franks of Jerusalem.
1241	**9 April**. Mongol defeat of western armies at Liegnitz.
1244	**23 August.** Jerusalem sacked by Khwarazmian mercenaries.
1249–50	Louis IX's Crusade attacks Egypt.
1250	**2 May.** Mamluks seize power in Egypt.
1258	Mongol sack of Baghdad.
1260	**3 September**. Mamluks defeat the Mongols at the Battle of Ain Jalut.
1268	Sultan Baibars captures Antioch.
1270	**25 August**. Louis IX dies near Tunis. His second crusade is abandoned.
1271–2	The Lord Edward of England in Acre.
1289	Mamluks capture Tripoli.
1291	Fall of Acre and of the remaining Frankish strongholds in the Crusader States.
1309	Knights of St John set up their headquarters in Rhodes.
1312	Pope Clement V dissolves the Order of the Temple.

1365	A crusade led by King Peter of Cyprus sacks Alexandria.
1386	Poland and Lithuania united. The effective end of the Prussian crusade.
1390	Crusade against Mahdia.
1396	**25 September**. Defeat of the crusade of Nicopolis by the Ottomans.
1415	Portuguese take Ceuta in Morocco.
1420–31	Unsuccessful crusades against the Hussites.
1444	**10 November**. Defeat of the crusade of Varna by the Ottomans.
1453	**29 May**. Ottoman Turks capture Constantinople.
1456	Relief of Belgrade; crusaders led by St John of Capistrano.
1492	Conquest of Granada by Ferdinand and Isabella.
1522	Ottoman conquest of Rhodes.
1530	Knights of St John move to Malta.
1565	Knights of St John at Malta defeat the armada of Sultan Suleyman.
1571	Ottomans conquer Cyprus. **7 October**. Fleet of the Holy League, led by Don John of Austria, defeats the Ottoman fleet at Lepanto.
1578	Death of King Sebastian of Portugal on crusade at Alcazar.
1683	Ottomans besiege Vienna unsuccessfully.
1684–99	Holy League recovers much of Hungary and Transylvania from the Ottomans.
1684–1715	Venice occupies much of the Peloponnese.
1798	Napoleon takes Malta from the Knights of St John.

PRUSS

Ma
PO
● 25 ✗

BOHEMIA

24 *Danu*

✗ 29 ●

● 1

● 2

3 ● ● 4

6 ● ● 5
8 7

Rhine

Garonne

Rhone

22

23

21

20

19

● 9

55 ●

PORTUGAL

CASTILE

ARAGON

● 10 ✗

● 11

13 12
✗

14

KINGDOM OF SICILY

15

16 ●

MALTA

17

KEY

Site of battle ✗

1. Paris	19. Naples	38. Nicaea
2. Cluny	20. Rome	39. Dorylaeum
3. Clermont	21. Pisa	40. Iconium
4. Lyons	22. Genoa	41. Attalia
5. Vienne	23. Venice	42. Antioch
6. Le Puy	24. Vienna	43. Aleppo
7. Albi	25. Liegnitz	44. Edessa
8. Toulouse	26. Marienburg	45. Manzikert
9. Barcelona	27. Riga	46. Mosul
10. Las Navas	28. Novgorod	47. Baghdad
de Tolosa	29. Mohács	48. Tripoli
11. Granada	30. Belgrade	49. Damascus
12. Ceuta	31. Nicopolis	50. Jerusalem
13. Alcazar	32. Varna	51. Damietta
14. Algiers	33. Kosovo	52. Cairo
15. Tunis	34. Durazzo	53. Mansurah
16. Mahdia	35. Lepanto	54. Alexandria
17. Tripoli	36. Constantinople	55. Lisbon
18. Otranto	37. Nicomedia	

THE WORLD OF THE CRUSADES

stonia   •28

7

NIA

ANIA

RUSSIA

asylvania

Wallachia

CAUCASUS

Caspian Sea

31   32
                  •45
•36
    •37   Euphrates
  38 •39   AZARBAIJAN

       40•   43•   •44   46•
                                Tigris
  41•   42   •47

RHODES   •48
          CYPRUS •49

                  •50

      54 51
            53
        52
   Nile

Introduction

Clermont Ferrand in late November seems an unlikely setting for the start of a world revolution. Yet it was there, in a meadow outside the cathedral, that on 27 November 1095 Pope Urban II preached his crusade sermon and set in motion a movement which was profoundly to affect western society for half a millennium. The crusades were part of an ongoing war between Christian and Muslim powers for the control of the Mediterranean, which began with the rise of Islam in the seventh century and has continued to the present day. What distinguished them from other phases of that war was a zeal for Jerusalem.

Jerusalem, sacred to Christians as the site of the Crucifixion, Resurrection and Ascension of Jesus, had, since the reign of the first Christian Roman Emperor, Constantine the Great (312–37), been a pilgrimage centre adorned with churches commemorating important events in the Gospels. But in 638 it was captured by the Caliph Omar, successor to the Prophet Muhammad (*c.* 570–632), founder of Islam. Muslims, like Christians, regarded Jerusalem as a holy city, because their Prophet had been taken there on a Night Journey by the Archangel Gabriel, had spoken there with the prophets who had preceded him, and then, from the living rock, had been carried to the throne of Allah in Paradise. His followers identified the platform of the Temple of Herod as the site of these events and built there the shrine known as the Dome of the Rock and the mosque of al-Aqsa.

Muhammad recognized Jesus as a prophet sent by God and limited toleration was therefore extended by his followers to Christians, but there was a lack of parity between the two faiths. Muhammad considered that Jesus and all the former prophets had received and taught the same revelation as himself, because Islam was the true religion; but that Christians had introduced many errors into his teaching. Christians were allowed to retain their churches and to worship freely by the Muslim authorities and forcible conversion was condemned, but they were treated as second-class citizens: they had to pay a religious poll tax, they were subject to discriminatory laws (e.g. they might not ride horses), and they were forbidden under penalty of death to criticize the Muslim religion or to seek to make Muslim converts. The Islamic rulers allowed Christian pilgrims to visit Jerusalem and the Holy Land, but few Western Christians did so before the tenth century.

Although divided politically and ethnically, Western Europe was united by membership of the Catholic Church, whose public worship was conducted in Latin, and whose chief bishop was the Pope. Virtually everyone in the West, apart from the Jews, was baptized and buried in accordance with Catholic rites and accepted the Christian picture of the universe and their place in it, even though they may have doubted specific parts of the faith. The Church taught an ideal of holiness based on world renunciation, the rejection of personal property and worldly success, the observance of chastity, and the subordination of the individual will to the teachings of the Gospels. These ideals contrasted starkly with the violence prevalent throughout much of Western society. Fighting men in particular (who included almost all the landowning classes) found the practice of the Christian life very difficult.

But in the period 950–1100 a religious revival took

place, spearheaded by some of the great monasteries like Cluny in Burgundy and supported by devout rulers. Its achievements were striking: the pagans of Scandinavia and of central and eastern Europe were converted to Catholicism, a network of parish churches began to be established throughout the 'old' Christian lands, and the reformers began to engage the consciences of some of the laity. Such men were faced with a dilemma. They could not all responsibly leave the world and become monks; yet although it was technically possible for a ruler or a warrior to live in an ascetic way, it was extremely difficult.

Pilgrimage provided a partial solution to the problem. Pilgrimages were not an obligatory part of Catholic observance, and were popular precisely because they were spontaneous expressions of lay piety. They involved some degree of self-denial, and to that extent conformed to contemporary ideals of holiness, but they did not require a permanent change of life. Many pilgrimages were made to local shrines but journeys to distant shrines like Rome and Compostela became quite common. Jerusalem was regarded as the holiest of all pilgrimage destinations and by AD 1000 it had become easier to reach. Western pilgrims could travel through Catholic lands to Belgrade where they entered the Orthodox Christian Empire of Byzantium which extended to northern Syria. Only the final stage of the journey was made through Muslim territory.

The pilgrims found Jerusalem an alien city, ruled by Muslims, and with many mosques from which the faithful were called to prayer five times each day. In 1009, in a rare act of intolerance, the Caliph Hakim of Egypt ordered the destruction of all Christian churches in the city, and although the Holy Sepulchre was rebuilt under Byzantine patronage by 1048, many of the other shrines remained in ruins. Moreover, those who had come to the Holy Land to follow in Christ's footsteps found that they were not allowed to process through the streets but could only worship behind the closed doors of their churches.

As pilgrimage to Jerusalem came to occupy a central role in the devotional aspirations of Western Christians, so resentment of Muslim rule in the Holy City grew. To understand this fully one should consider how modern Muslims would feel if their holy city of Mecca had been captured by a Western power, which, while protecting the Muslim shrines and permitting the *haj* to take place, also built many Christian churches in the city and regarded Islam with disdain. However, before 1095 Western Christians were powerless to remedy the situation: sheer distance ruled out political intervention and individual visitors could take no action because pilgrims were required to travel unarmed.

ONE

The First Crusade

In 1071 the Seljuk Sultan of Baghdad defeated the main Byzantine field army at Manzikert in eastern Asia Minor and during the next few years Turkish warbands occupied most of the Asiatic provinces of Byzantium. This made it hazardous for Western pilgrims to make the pilgrimage to Jerusalem unless they were rich enough to pay a large, armed escort. But in the 1090s the Turkish Empire was weakened by faction. It was an ideal time for Byzantine intervention and the Emperor Alexius I (1081–1118) appealed to the Pope for help in recruiting Western knights to serve as mercenaries in his armies.

This was the catalyst which led the Pope to launch the First Crusade. Urban II (1088–99) was in the middle of a bitter and prolonged dispute with the Western Emperor, Henry IV (1056–1106) about the control of Church appointments. Henry had set up an antipope in 1080 and the Church in his dominions did not acknowledge Urban's authority. In 1095 Urban visited France to preside over a Church council at Clermont. As he travelled there he sounded out the opinion of senior churchmen and noblemen about the crusade and met with a favourable response.

Urban was a Frenchman and preached to the crowds outside Clermont cathedral on 27 November in their own language. He took up Alexius's appeal for fighting men to aid their Eastern brethren against the Turks but he developed this theme, urging them to go on and liberate the Holy City of Jerusalem, and he offered them a spiritual reward:

> Whoever for devotion alone, not to gain honour or money, goes to Jerusalem to liberate the Church of God, can substitute this journey for all penance.

This crusading indulgence was arguably the chief incentive of those who took the cross. All fighting men were members of the Church and bound by its rules. If they committed serious sins, particularly sins of violence, they were required to feel remorse in their hearts, to make confession to a priest, and to perform the penance enjoined on them, in order to obtain forgiveness. But traditional penances were incompatible with a warrior's self-image for they usually involved bread-and-water fasts and acts of public humiliation. So many delayed making their confession. But that was a calculated risk, since to die unabsolved was to risk damnation, and for a warrior death was an ever-present hazard.

Urban's crusade indulgence allowed knights to substitute military service for all other penances prescribed for all past sins which they had confessed. The Pope was aware of the problems which warriors experienced because he came from a family of fighting men, and he encouraged them to practise the Christian life by using their fighting skills and aggressive instincts in the service of God. All they needed to do was to make a solemn vow in the presence of a priest, confess their sins to him, and wear a red cross on their cloaks. The crusade indulgence was not an easy way out: the majority of those who went on the First Crusade were killed, whereas a traditional penance, such as a bread-and-water fast, would not have been at all life threatening. The crusade was, however, immensely popular. When Urban finished speaking the crowd shouted, 'God wills it, God wills it', and surged forward to take the cross.

Urban envisaged a single expedition and appointed as its leader and his representative Bishop Adhémar of Le Puy, who had been a knight before he was ordained. News of the crusade was carried to other parts of Europe by delegates from the council returning home, by preachers commissioned by the Pope, and by Urban himself, who toured France seeking recruits.

The movement soon moved outside the Pope's control. It was preached in northern France by unauthorized men like Peter the Hermit, who appealed to all social classes, inspiring his followers with an apocalyptic vision of the victory which God would give them because of their faith, not because of their strength. Such preaching produced the movement known as the Peasants' Crusade (although some knights and many artisans also joined it) which contained huge numbers of non-combatants. They travelled to Constantinople in 1096 and against the Emperor's advice crossed to Asia Minor and offered battle to the Turks. The majority were massacred or enslaved, although some 3,000 survived and joined the main crusade.

Until recently the motives ascribed to the fighting men who took the cross were based partly on anecdotal evidence and largely on conjecture. Economic motives were reckoned to have been very important, particularly the desire of younger sons of knightly birth to make their fortunes in the East. Undoubtedly that was true of some crusaders, including some of the leaders, but recent research has shown that the majority of the participants of noble birth were men with well-established positions in the West, lords or elder sons who were motivated to crusade by religious zeal rather than by secular concerns. Of course few of them can have had unmixed motives, and a love of fighting for its own sake should not be underestimated, but far from seeking lands in the East the majority of crusader knights wished to return home.

Many non-combatants, including many women, took the cross and set out with the main armies, seeing in the crusade an opportunity to make the pilgrimage to Jerusalem with strong military protection. Urban's attempts to discourage them were largely ignored. In the late summer of 1096 five armies left the West for Constantinople. Godfrey of Bouillon, Duke of Lower Lorraine, led an army from the Rhineland and Frisia by the overland route. The Pope's legate, Bishop

Adhémar, was joined at Le Puy by Count Raymond IV of Toulouse and an army of southern Frenchmen, and they marched to Byzantium through Lombardy and Dalmatia. Three other armies crossed the Adriatic from the ports of south Italy: the first was led by Hugh of Vermandois, brother of the King of France; the second was a force of south Italian Normans led by Bohemond of Otranto; the third was led by Duke Robert of Normandy (eldest son of William the Conqueror) and Count Robert of Flanders.

There are no precise statistics for the First Crusade, but John France has plausibly estimated that the numbers at the start of the campaign were some 50–60,000. The Emperor Alexius handled very skilfully the challenge posed by large, independent armies marching through his territory. The crusade leaders recognized that they were dependent on the emperor's goodwill for basic necessities like food and fodder and they reluctantly accepted the terms which he imposed on them. They undertook to return any lands which had once formed part of his empire and to hold any other territory they might conquer as his vassals. Their armies were then ferried across the Bosphorus to the Imperial military base outside Nicomedia.

The crusaders' reactions to the Byzantines were ambivalent. They expected to be welcomed as deliverers from the Turks and were outraged when the Greeks viewed them with suspicion and refused to let them live off the land. The Byzantine court looked down on the crusaders as uncouth barbarians, while the crusaders, although they were impressed by the wealth and high civilization of the Byzantine capital, regarded the Byzantine aristocrats as effeminate because they employed professional troops to fight for them.

Sultan Kilij-Arslan, the chief Turkish ruler in Asia Minor, refused to return from a campaign on his eastern frontier, thinking that the princes' crusade was another undisciplined rabble like the Peasants' Crusade before it. So with Byzantine help the crusaders were able to capture the sultan's capital, Nicaea, and to advance into central Anatolia. They met the army of Kilij-Arslan at Dorylaeum and were disconcerted by Turkish battle tactics. The Turks were lightly armed, mounted archers, who used encirclement to wear down their enemy and were not vulnerable to the Western cavalry charge, which they let through their lines without harm to themselves. Nevertheless, the crusaders won the battle, largely because of an outflanking movement led by Bishop Adhémar. Thereafter the way to Syria lay relatively open.

Emperor Alexius assigned his trusted general Taticius to the crusade. The general may have been a culture shock to the crusaders – he was a eunuch with a golden nose – but he and his staff knew the road system of Asia Minor (the crusaders had no maps), and were able to liaise with the Armenian Christian princes who had carved out independent principalities in the Taurus and anti-Taurus mountains. Their help was crucial because it enabled the crusaders to send a detachment to secure the ports on the Cilician and north Syrian coasts, thus linking their armies to the outside world again, and to convey the main force to northern Syria in safety without the danger of a Turkish ambush.

The crusaders did not face a united Muslim opposition in Syria. Power was divided between Prince Ridwan of Aleppo and his brother, Prince Duqaq of Damascus, who were enemies, while the governors of many of the great cities were virtually independent. The crusade's first objective was to capture Antioch, which was very strongly fortified.

They besieged the city from October 1097 until June 1098, and only gained entrance through the treachery of one of the garrison commanders. Almost immediately they were themselves besieged by a large relief army from Mosul. Because there were no stores of food in Antioch, the crusaders decided to give battle rather than face starvation behind the walls, and with the courage of desperation under the brilliant command of Prince Bohemond they scored a notable victory over a numerically superior Islamic force on 28 June 1098.

Alexius and his army had remained in western Asia Minor, occupying whole provinces in the wake of Kilij-Arslan's defeat by the crusade. When deserters from the siege of Antioch informed the emperor that the crusade was doomed, rather than hastening to help them he returned to Constantinople. When the crusaders learned of this, they considered themselves absolved from their oaths of allegiance to Alexius because he had failed in the primary duty of a lord, that of giving aid to his vassals. They therefore refused to hand over to him Antioch or any other conquests which they made.

The Fatimid Caliphate of Cairo, which had a strong fleet and held most of the ports on the Syrian coast south of Tripoli, was able to profit from the defeat which the crusade had inflicted on the Turkish powers in Syria. In 1098 the Fatimids evicted the Turkish garrisons from the inland cities of Palestine, including Jerusalem, and offered the crusaders a military alliance against the Turks together with free access for all pilgrims who wished to visit Jerusalem, but such a proposal was of no interest to the crusaders. They rejected it, and in May 1099 crossed the Fatimid frontier and marched towards Jerusalem.

Their military strength had been depleted by the garrisons they had left in Antioch and other captured cities and they were concerned to reach Jerusalem before the Fatimids could move their main army from Egypt to oppose them. The crusaders therefore marched straight down the coast, making no attempt to capture any of the cities they passed. They reached Jerusalem on 6 June 1099 and succeeded in forcing a way into the city on 15 July. The Fatimid governor, fearing treachery, had expelled all the Christian inhabitants before the siege began but the Jews of Jerusalem fought alongside the Muslims to defend their homes. The crusaders celebrated their victory by slaughtering the entire population before fulfilling their vows by praying at the Holy Sepulchre. As the twentieth century has shown, prolonged warfare breeds atrocities of that kind.

Soon after the capture of Jerusalem the Egyptian relief army landed at Ascalon. The crusaders once again confronted an enemy whose tactics were unknown to them. In fact, the massed battle formation which the Fatimids favoured was very vulnerable to a charge by heavily mailed Western cavalrymen, and the battle fought on 12 August was a notable crusader victory. Against all odds the First Crusade had been successful. The volunteer army, encumbered by non-combatants, had marched thousands of miles, defeated the main Turkish and Egyptian field armies, and restored the Holy City of Jerusalem to Christian rule for the first time in 450 years.

TWO

Foundation of the Crusader States

In the aftermath of the First Crusade its leaders elected Godfrey of Bouillon as Advocate of the Holy Sepulchre, a title of honour given to lay defenders of Church property. John France has estimated that some 20,000 participants survived the crusade, of whom some 3,000 remained in Jerusalem with Godfrey and another 3,000 probably stayed in north Syria. The rest returned home in the autumn of 1099.

The conquests made by the crusade had been haphazard. In the north the Franks held the County of Edessa which in 1097 had been ruled by Prince Thoros, an Armenian, who appealed to the crusade for help against the Turks as it marched to Antioch. Godfrey of Bouillon's brother, Baldwin, rode to Edessa with eighty knights and was adopted by Thoros as his heir. When Thoros was killed in a riot a few months later, Baldwin became Count of Edessa, a province with defined boundaries and a class of Armenian landowners. Meanwhile, Bohemond, who had become Prince of Antioch (1098–1111), ruled the coastal regions of Cilicia and Syria as far south as Latakia, together with a few inland cities, but the two northern states were separated from the Franks of Jerusalem by a broad tract of Muslim territory.

Godfrey of Bouillon ruled Jerusalem only for a year (1099–1100), during which time Galilee was conquered and the port of Haifa secured with Venetian help. He was succeeded by his brother, Baldwin of Edessa, who in turn appointed his cousin, Baldwin of Le Bourg, to succeed him as Count of Edessa. Baldwin I (1100–18) did not intend to be subordinate to the Church as Godfrey had been: he rejected the title of advocate and was crowned king on Christmas Day 1100 in the church of the Holy Nativity at Bethlehem.

All the Frankish states were acutely short of manpower. However, a new crusade was being organized in the West consisting chiefly of those who had not yet fulfilled the vows they had taken in 1095–6. Contemporaries estimated that almost as many people took part in this as in the First Crusade. Three separate armies entered Asia Minor in 1101 and all were decisively defeated by the Turks who were reinforced by troops from Aleppo. The few survivors made their way to Jerusalem where they helped Baldwin I to repel an Egyptian invasion but most then returned to the West and the manpower problems of the Latin East remained unresolved.

THE KINGDOM OF JERUSALEM, 1101–31

The Caliphs of Cairo sought to recover Jerusalem and in 1101, 1102 and 1105 large Fatimid armies came to Palestine. Despite their superior numbers they were beaten by the heavily mailed Frankish cavalry. Meanwhile, Baldwin I made the reduction of the coastal cities his priority. The Fatimids would be deprived of bases if he succeeded; his revenues would be boosted; and war supplies and pilgrims would be able to reach the Franks from the West with minimum hindrance. From the foundation of the kingdom pilgrims flocked to Jerusalem in huge numbers, and it was from these visitors that the Frankish rulers recruited settlers and fighting men.

The Franks had no navy of their own but the Italian maritime cities assisted them in capturing the ports. Before the First Crusade eastern Mediterranean trade had been dominated by the Venetians who held a privileged trading position in the Byzantine Empire. The republics of Genoa and Pisa were anxious to share in the luxury goods trade of the Levant, and the Venetians too were interested in extending their influence. As a result all three powers were willing to help the nascent Crusader States. By 1110, apart from Tyre and Ascalon, the entire coast from the Sinai to Cilicia was in crusader hands.

Baldwin faced no sustained threat from Damascus which was intermittently at war with Aleppo and made peace with Jerusalem in 1108 establishing a negotiated frontier in eastern Galilee. In 1115 Baldwin occupied Transjordan and fortified the port of Eilat but made no attempt to gain control of the caravan routes in the Syrian desert because the Franks never mastered the art of using camels in warfare.

Marriage alliances became important too. Baldwin's first wife and their young children had died during the crusade. His second marriage to an Armenian princess was childless and it was dissolved;

she went to live in Constantinople. Then in 1112 Baldwin married the Dowager Countess Adelaide of Sicily who brought him a rich dowry and their marriage settlement stipulated that her son, Roger II, would succeed in Jerusalem if Baldwin died without issue. In 1117, under pressure from his vassals, Baldwin had this marriage annulled on the grounds that his second wife was still living. This must have been known to both parties in 1112 and both must then have been convinced that Baldwin's Armenian marriage had been validly dissolved. In fact it seems likely that the annulment proceedings of 1117 were designed to exclude Roger of Sicily from the succession. Roger never forgave the way in which the Franks had humiliated his mother and refused to give them any help throughout his long reign in spite of the fact that Sicily remained the nearest Catholic power to the Kingdom of Jerusalem.

With Roger II eliminated from the succession, Baldwin was followed on the throne in 1118 by his cousin, Baldwin of Le Bourg, Count of Edessa, who became King Baldwin II (1118–31), and appointed his own cousin, Joscelin I of Courtenay, as Count of Edessa. During his reign Tyre was captured in 1124 with Venetian help; this victory restricted the range of the Fatimid fleet, and it became comparatively safe for Western shipping to sail to the Holy Land by way of the Greek islands and Cyprus.

THE NORTHERN STATES TO 1131

From the beginning of his reign in Antioch, Bohemond was attacked simultaneously by Aleppo from the east and by Byzantium from the west, because Alexius I wanted to restore Byzantine rule in the principality. In 1105 Bohemond appointed his nephew, Tancred (d. 1112), as regent, returned to the West and persuaded Pope Paschal II (1099–1118) to preach a new crusade. This was well supported and Bohemond deployed it against the Byzantine Empire, besieging the Adriatic port of Durazzo. However, he was defeated and forced to make an humiliating peace in 1108. He retired to south Italy and died there in 1111, but Tancred profited from the diversion of Byzantine forces to the west, recovered all the lost territories and stabilized his eastern frontier.

By this time a fourth Frankish state had come into being, the County of Tripoli, which linked the Kingdom of Jerusalem to the Principality of Antioch, and which had been conquered by Raymond IV of

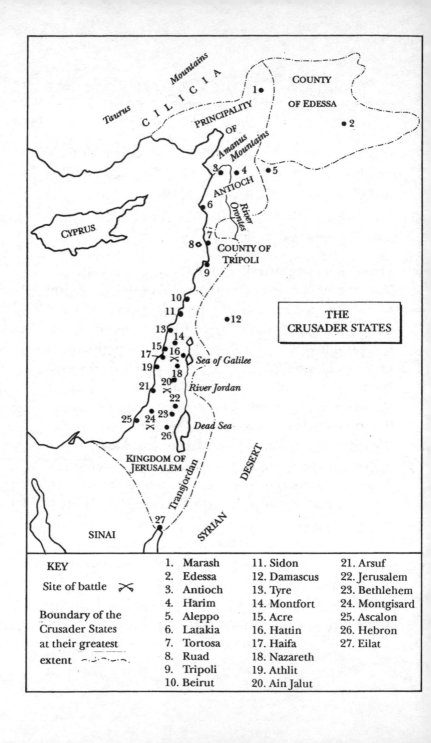

THE
CRUSADER STATES

KEY

Site of battle ✕

Boundary of the
Crusader States
at their greatest

extent ⌐·⌐·⌐·

1. Marash
2. Edessa
3. Antioch
4. Harim
5. Aleppo
6. Latakia
7. Tortosa
8. Ruad
9. Tripoli
10. Beirut

11. Sidon
12. Damascus
13. Tyre
14. Montfort
15. Acre
16. Hattin
17. Haifa
18. Nazareth
19. Athlit
20. Ain Jalut

21. Arsuf
22. Jerusalem
23. Bethlehem
24. Montgisard
25. Ascalon
26. Hebron
27. Eilat

Toulouse (d. 1105) and his son Bertrand. It now became possible for the Franks to take concerted action against a common enemy. This soon became essential, for the growth of Frankish power in Syria alarmed the Muslims of Iraq and Mawdud of Mosul led a *jihad* against them annually from 1110 to 1113. Although Mawdud inflicted great damage, he made no conquests because all four Frankish rulers combined to resist him and Ridwan of Aleppo refused to cooperate with him, fearing Mawdud's success might jeopardize his own independence. Ridwan protected the members of an extremist Shi'ite sect, the Nizarite Ismailis, whom the Franks called the Assassins. They sought to create a pan-Islamic revolution and because they were few in number, they used political assassination to forward their aims. Among their victims was Mawdud, whom they stabbed in the great mosque of Damascus in 1113, thus bringing the *jihad* to an abrupt end and involuntarily helping the Franks.

After Ridwan died in 1113 Aleppo was torn by faction and Tancred's successor, Prince Roger of Antioch, was able to seize large parts of its territory. In 1119 the Aleppans placed their government in the hands of the Turkish Prince Il-Ghazi, who in alliance with Damascus invaded Antioch, annihilated the Frankish army and killed Prince Roger at the Battle of the Field of Blood. The Aleppans were able to recover much of their lost territory but could not exploit their victory fully because of the prompt intervention of Baldwin II, who became regent of Antioch on behalf of Bohemond's young son, Bohemond II.

Baldwin reorganized the defences of Antioch, and after Il-Ghazi died in 1122 it became evident that there was no longer a real crisis in Frankish north Syria. Indeed although Baldwin II and Joscelin I of Edessa were both captured by the Turks in minor skirmishes in 1123, no attempt was made by the Muslims to exploit the fact that Antioch and Edessa were left leaderless. The only price Baldwin had to pay was a large ransom.

In 1126 the sixteen-year-old Bohemond II came to Syria and Baldwin was able to return to Jerusalem. Bohemond was popular with his subjects but in 1130 was killed while campaigning in Cilicia, leaving only an infant daughter to succeed him. During her minority the Armenians of the Taurus Mountains seized the Cilician plain and its cities, depriving Antioch of one of its richest provinces.

By the time Baldwin II died in 1131, the Franks, although they had failed to capture Aleppo and Damascus and were therefore vulnerable to an attack from the east, had nevertheless conquered an impressive amount of territory. Their lands extended from Edessa in Mesopotamia in the east to the Mediterranean coast at Antioch, and from Marash in the anti-Taurus Mountains in the north to Eilat and the Sinai peninsula. By 1131 the Franks arguably benefited from the fact that their territories formed a buffer between the Fatimid Caliphate of Egypt and the Turkish warlords of Syria and Iraq.

THREE

Twelfth-Century Crusader Society

The Franks in the Crusader States ruled over a very racially diverse population. However, it was not ethnic differences which bothered them but religious ones. The Franks themselves were drawn from all parts of Western Europe and all they had in common was membership of the Catholic Church: they therefore defined themselves as 'Christians of the Roman observance'. Consequently anybody of free birth who was prepared to be received into the Catholic Church, whatever his ethnic or religious background, enjoyed social and legal parity with the Franks. Some people of other faiths made the change, but the majority remained true to their own religious traditions. The Franks were therefore always in a minority. In the Kingdom of Jerusalem they made up about 20 per cent of the population by 1180, but they were probably a smaller minority still in the northern states.

All Franks were treated in law as free men and

women, even though many first generation settlers may have been serfs in Western Europe. All non-noble Franks were given the status of burgess which reflected the fact that most lived in towns or in the new settlements which grew up around castles. There were a few Frankish villages, but they were exceptional.

GOVERNMENT

Each of the four Crusader States was autonomous, even though the Counts of Tripoli and Edessa acknowledged the overlordship of the King of Jerusalem. The governments of all the states were similar, though not identical, and only that of Jerusalem will be described here.

The part of the kingdom which made up the royal demesne was under the direct rule of the king, the rest was divided into lordships, held in military tenure by the king's vassals. The king and his vassals granted parts of their lands to subtenants in return for military service (a process known as sub-infeudation), but few of the subtenants were men of any consequence and most were simple knights. Moreover, because good agricultural land was in short supply, many knights did not hold land at all but were granted money fiefs, in effect annual salaries paid from the commercial dues of the cities. Such men, although they enjoyed the social status and legal privileges of noblemen, were not rich.

All those who held land from the king in military tenure were entitled to attend his council, known in Jerusalem as the High Court, but only the great lords normally did so. The king chose his officers of state from this group (apart from the chancellor who was always a churchman). The most important officers were the seneschal, who had charge of the treasury and deputized for the king if the need arose, the constable, who was commander-in-chief of the army under the king, and the chamberlain, who had charge of the king's privy purse.

The High Court dealt with all legal business involving the king's vassals and had power to enact laws but its chief function was to advise the king on matters of state. When the king wished to consult a wider spectrum of opinion he invited representatives of the Church, the military orders, the merchant communities and the Frankish burgesses together with the members of the High Court to a General Court (*curia generalis*).

Much of the power in the kingdom was devolved

to the royal vassals. Each lord had a court attended by his own vassals, with authority over the noble Franks in the lordship. In each lordship there was also at least one burgess court, presided over by a viscount whom the lord appointed, which could judge all cases involving Frankish burgesses and all criminal cases involving non-Franks. An identical system of courts existed in the royal demesne. These local courts could impose the death sentence and there was no right of appeal from them. The only cases they were not competent to judge were ecclesiastical ones (including marriage disputes), which were heard by the Church courts, and offences reserved to the crown, such as theft committed by children.

THE NON-FRANKISH POPULATION

Many of the Franks' subjects were Muslims. Although the crusaders massacred the Muslims of Jerusalem in 1099 and those of Arsuf in 1101, these were exceptional cases. The majority of the Muslim population in other cities which the Franks captured were expelled but granted safe conduct into Muslim territory. Some were even allowed to stay. In the countryside the Franks evicted Muslim landlords but were anxious to conciliate the Muslim peasantry because they needed a contented labour force. Peasants were required to pay a religious poll tax, but were allowed complete religious freedom and almost no attempt was made to convert them to Christianity. Muslim villages continued to be run by their own headmen and civil disputes between villagers continued to be settled in accordance with Islamic law.

Jewish communities were also required to pay a religious poll tax but kept their synagogues and rabbinic schools and civil disputes among them were settled in accordance with Talmudic law. However, although the Franks allowed them to visit Jerusalem and pray at the Western Wall, only a few Jewish families were allowed to live in the Holy City.

The Franks granted religious toleration to all the many Eastern Christians in their lands and freed them from the payment of poll tax. Eastern Christians were allowed to keep their own property and to regulate their own ecclesiastical affairs and their leaders were permitted to deal with civil disputes among members of their communities in the customary way. They belonged to four main churches: the Armenian, Jacobite, Maronite and the Byzantine Orthodox. The Franks were on excellent terms with the first three groups, and indeed some of the Maronites entered into full communion with the papacy in about 1181. But the Byzantine Orthodox proved a problem. The Franks considered Byzantine Christians to be members of their own Catholic Church and while not interfering with their forms of service, canon law or property rights made them subject to Catholic bishops. The Byzantine Orthodox resented this subservience and were encouraged in this by the emperors in Constantinople.

THE ECONOMY

Frankish landlords lived in towns or castles and employed salaried officials to supervise the peasantry on their estates. They treated all peasants as serfs and normally required them to render between a quarter and a third of their produce; but except in the case of landlords who owned vineyards or sugar plantations, the peasants were not required to perform labour services and even in those exceptional cases the services required were very light.

The wealth of the kingdom was in trade, not agriculture, and this was developed by merchants from the Italian maritime republics with whose help the ports had been captured. In return for their support the Frankish rulers had signed treaties with the republics granting them quarters in the ports consisting of one or more streets with houses, warehouses, and public buildings including a church. Such colonies functioned rather as embassy compounds do now; they were under the authority of magistrates appointed by the home cities and largely exempt from royal jurisdiction. In addition each republic enjoyed partial or total exemption from the payment of tariffs on some or all imports and exports in one or more cities.

The Italian fleets sailed to Syria and the Holy Land twice yearly, in spring and midsummer, bringing large numbers of pilgrims and cargoes of iron and timber, needed as war supplies, and woollen textiles which had a market in the Islamic world as well as among the Franks. The ports of the Crusader States were also an outlet for the trade of Damascus and Aleppo, which were the western terminals of trade routes stretching to India and the Far East. In addition the Italian fleets exported sugar produced in the Crusader Kingdom, for which there was a growing Western market, and luxury goods obtained from Islamic merchants, such as Arab gold work, Damascene metalwork, Persian carpets and ceramics, spices and medical drugs from the Indies, and Chinese silk.

Although customs dues formed an important part of the royal revenue, the exemptions granted to Italian merchants did not impoverish the crown unduly. The Italians did not normally travel to the Islamic cities of the interior, but instead Muslim merchants had to come and trade with them, and Muslims, of course, were not exempt from any of the tariffs on imports and exports.

DEFENCE

The Crusader States were continually at war. The Franks built many castles and although some of them served as administrative centres, they all had an important role in the defence of the kingdom. The field army was not large. In about 1180 the King of Jerusalem was owed the service of some 655 knights by his vassals and 5,025 sergeants by the Catholic Church and the cities. Sergeants were lightly mailed troops who might be deployed either as cavalry or infantry. To bulk out these forces in times of crisis, the crown recruited mercenaries drawn from knights and other soldiers of fortune who had come from the West. It also called upon Turcopoles, a light cavalry force recruited from the native population both Christian and Muslim. The northern states had their own armies, although no comparable details about them are known. Although large armies of 15,000 to 20,000 troops could be mustered according to need by the kings of Jerusalem, these additional men had to be paid and that was a severe strain on the resources of a comparatively small, not very rich kingdom. It was this that made the military orders so important.

The Knights Templar, founded in 1119 by Hugh de Payens and licensed as a religious order in 1128 by Honorius II, took their name from their headquarters in the al-Aqsa mosque which they believed stood on the site of Solomon's Temple. They took the traditional monastic vows of poverty, chastity and obedience but devoted their lives to fighting in defence of the faith rather than to contemplative prayer. They thus gave institutional expression to the crusading ideal. All brethren had to be bachelors or widowers and the order admitted knights, sergeants, and priests who served as chaplains. Power was vested in the knights; they elected the master, who had no religious superior but the Pope. The order rapidly grew and received endowments of property in the East and all over Western Europe.

The Knights of St John had been founded as an order to care for the sick and poor, which is why they are often called the Knights Hospitaller, but at some time before 1150 they assumed military duties as well.

Both orders had their headquarters in Jerusalem and came to resemble each other quite closely. The Templar knights wore white cloaks with red crosses and the Knights of St John black cloaks with white crosses. Members of both orders were full-time professional soldiers, trained to obey orders, unlike lay knights who were amateurs and difficult to discipline on the battlefield. During the twelfth century the orders took a major role in the defence of Antioch and Tripoli where they were granted palatinate lordships. In the Kingdom of Jerusalem, although they held some castles, their importance lay more in the contribution they made to the field army. By the 1180s the two orders combined could muster a force of some 600 knights, equal in size to that provided by the king's lay vassals. Their services cost the crown nothing but they were the king's allies, not his subjects. He could not count on their automatic support when he campaigned outside the kingdom but he did enjoy their unconditional loyalty if the kingdom was attacked.

FRANKISH SOCIETY

By the middle of the twelfth century the scattered conquests of the First Crusade had been melded into a coherent group of states with a Frankish ruling class which outwardly appeared very Western: they were all Latin Catholics and they spoke French – the French of Paris in Jerusalem and Edessa, the French of Toulouse in Tripoli, and Norman French at Antioch. Although some of the high nobility married Byzantine or Armenian princesses, most tended to marry among themselves, or to fetch husbands and wives from the West. Many poor knights and Frankish burgesses married Eastern Christians, and their children took their father's religion and status. Marriage or sexual relations of any kind with Muslims were forbidden by law, unless the Muslim had first been baptized.

Most Franks in the Crusader States enjoyed a better standard of living than their kinsfolk in the West. They lived in stone houses and had a more varied diet, and while retaining Western fashions of dress, had a wider choice of fabrics, like cotton and silk which were prohibitively expensive in northern Europe.

Because this society was always at war, male death rates were high and as a consequence power had to be delegated to noblewomen. They were allowed to inherit fiefs in default of male heirs; mothers rather than the king were normally the legal guardians for minor heirs; and heiresses could not be married arbitrarily by the crown but had to be offered a choice of three suitors, none of whom should be disparaging to them in rank. Some Italian merchants did try to imitate Muslim practice and keep their wives in strict seclusion, but this was unusual.

THE HOLY CITY

The Catholic Church was established in the Crusader States for the use of the 'Christians of the

Roman observance' under Latin Patriarchs of
Antioch and Jerusalem, each assisted by suffragan
bishops. Catholic parish churches and chapels were
only built in towns and rural areas where Franks
lived but the principal shrine churches, in places
like Nazareth and Bethlehem, were entrusted to
Catholic clergy.

The First Crusade had been launched to liberate
Jerusalem, and the Franks turned it into a Catholic
city. The ruined shrine churches outside the walls
were all rebuilt and were served by religious
communities. The Church of the Holy Sepulchre was
enlarged by the addition of a Gothic cathedral to the
Byzantine rotunda, thus linking the sites of Christ's
Crucifixion and Resurrection and the shrine of the
Holy Cross within a single complex. Jerusalem
became an entirely Christian city and one in which,
although the Eastern Christians all had churches, the
Catholic Church predominated. Visitors from the
West could see the events of the Gospels liturgically
reenacted on the very sites where they had occurred
by Catholic clergy using familiar forms of service.
The impact of crusader Jerusalem on Catholic piety
awoke in Western Europe a strong devotion to the
humanity of Christ.

FOUR

Muslim Counter-Offensive

Once the Franks were firmly established in the Levant they proved very difficult to dislodge. The first serious threat to their security came in 1128 when Zengi, the governor of Mosul, was invited to become ruler of Aleppo. Initially he was involved in wars with other Muslim powers and then was deterred from attacking the Franks by the intervention of the Byzantine Emperor John II (1118–43). Between 1137 and 1143 he campaigned twice in north Syria seeking to regain control of Antioch and although he did not succeed, Zengi was intimidated by the power of the Byzantine army and refrained from attacking the Franks himself.

But when John died in a hunting accident in 1143 and his heir, Manuel, returned to Constantinople to be crowned, Zengi was free to attack the Franks, and on Christmas Eve 1144 he captured Edessa after a brief siege. This was the most serious set-back which the Franks in the East had yet suffered and it prompted Pope Eugenius III (1145–53) to launch the Second Crusade.

This crusade was preached by St Bernard of Clairvaux and met with an enormous response. At Easter 1146 King Louis VII of France (1137–80), his wife, Eleanor of Aquitaine, and many French noblemen took the cross, and at Christmas of that year the Western Emperor Conrad III (1138–52) and his nephew, the future Emperor Frederick Barbarossa, followed suit, together with many of their vassals. Both the German and French armies took the land route to Constantinople in 1147, while an English and Flemish crusading fleet set out by sea but was diverted by the King of Portugal to capture Lisbon from the Moors and never reached the Holy Land. The crusade received no military help from the Byzantine Emperor Manuel (1143–80) who was preoccupied by the invasion of his empire by Roger II of Sicily; this forced him to make peace with the Turkish Sultan of Iconium.

The German army tried to march through Turkish territory and suffered a catastrophic defeat in November 1147. The survivors either joined the French army or went to the Holy Land by sea. The

French made their way to Attalia, where Louis VII and his knights took ship to Antioch, but the infantry marched along the coast to Syria and suffered heavy losses. Nevertheless, the number of crusaders who reached Syria in 1148 was not negligible. King Louis and his knights were anxious to visit the Holy Places and ignoring the pleas of Prince Raymond of Antioch that they should attack Aleppo left for the south, where at a great assembly of the crusader leaders and the Frankish barons it was decided to attack the independent Muslim state of Damascus. Had they succeeded, the Crusader States would have been more secure, but the campaign was a fiasco and Damascus, hitherto a friendly power, was alienated. This marked the effective end of the Second Crusade which had achieved nothing at great cost in human lives.

Zengi had been murdered in 1146, and his two sons divided their inheritance: Saif ad-Din took Mosul, Nur ad-Din Aleppo and Edessa. Shielded by his brother from involvement with other Muslim powers, Nur ad-Din could concentrate on attacking the Franks. In 1149 he mounted an invasion of Antioch during which Prince Raymond was killed. Nur ad-Din subsequently annexed most of the

Frankish territories to the east and north of the River Orontes.

The Kingdom of Jerusalem was unaffected by these disasters in the north and in 1153 King Baldwin III (1143–63) captured Ascalon, the last Egyptian-held port in Palestine, after a long siege. But in 1154 Nur ad-Din annexed Damascus, and the Zengid princes, who between them ruled a great arc of territory from Mosul to the borders of eastern Galilee, then posed a threat to all the Franks.

Nur ad-Din was unable to exploit this advantage because in 1159 the Byzantine Emperor Manuel brought a large army to Antioch where Prince Reynald and Baldwin III of Jerusalem recognized him as their overlord. Manuel then led an expedition against Aleppo and Nur ad-Din was overawed by his power, but Manuel had no wish to conduct a lengthy war in Syria. He made peace with Nur ad-Din in return for his help against the Turkish Sultan of Iconium and then returned to Constantinople.

During the 1160s the focus of political interest in the Near East shifted to Egypt where rival viziers appealed for support to Nur ad-Din and to King Amalric of Jerusalem (1163–74). Nur ad-Din delegated the conduct of the Egyptian wars to his general Shirkuh who was accompanied on campaign by his nephew Saladin. Initially Nur ad-Din was able to divert Amalric's attention by attacking Frankish territory while the king was in Egypt, forcing him to bring his army back to Palestine. Thus in 1164 Nur ad-Din captured the key fortress of Harim, near Antioch, and defeated a relief army led by Bohemond III of Antioch and Raymond III of Tripoli, both of whom were taken prisoner. Yet because he feared Byzantine reprisals, Nur ad-Din did not follow through his victory. In 1165 he released Bohemond in return for a large ransom, which Manuel paid. This left Amalric free to continue campaigning in Egypt which was a necessity because a victory for Shirkuh would have led to an immense increase in Nur ad-Din's power.

In 1167 Amalric forced Shirkuh to withdraw from Egypt and the Fatimid Caliph agreed to pay an annual subsidy of 100,000 dinars and to accept a Frankish garrison and a Frankish Resident in Cairo. The settlement was very unpopular and in 1168 Amalric resolved to impose direct rule on Egypt. This prompted the Egyptians to turn once again to Nur ad-Din for help. Shirkuh was victorious over the

Franks and took over the government himself, being appointed vizier by the Caliph of Cairo. When he died early in 1169 his nephew, Saladin, succeeded him as vizier. However, when the Caliph of Cairo died in 1171 Saladin did not allow a successor to be appointed, but restored Egypt to the spiritual obedience of the Caliph of Baghdad and ruled as Nur ad-Din's representative. In the following years he strengthened his own position by annexing Cyrenaica and the Yemen, and took Eilat from the Franks in 1171. But he would not join with Nur ad-Din in attacking the Franks of Jerusalem, seeming to prefer to keep them as a buffer between himself and the court of Damascus.

Nur ad-Din died on 15 May 1174 and his generals struggled over the regency for his eleven-year-old son, as-Salih. The Franks could not take advantage of the feuding because King Amalric died shortly after on 11 July 1174, leaving a thirteen-year-old son, Baldwin IV (1174–85), who had been diagnosed as suffering from leprosy. A struggle for the regency in Jerusalem followed, enabling Saladin to move his army from Egypt and to capture Damascus without meeting any opposition from the Franks. It was Saladin's ambition to unite all the Zengid lands under his own rule, although he had no title whatsoever to them and had to dispossess Nur ad-Din's family in order to succeed. He justified his actions by claiming that his real desire was to unite all Muslims in the Near East so that he might lead a *jihad* against the Franks and recover Jerusalem for Islam. His piety may have been sincere but his ambition was undoubted, and this made him a very dangerous enemy to the Franks.

The government of Jerusalem was divided about how to deal with the threat. Raymond of Tripoli, the regent, believed the best policy was to keep peace with Saladin, but this was a highly dangerous strategy for it would allow him to become powerful and then to attack the Frankish states at a time of his own choosing. The young King Baldwin, who came of age at fifteen in 1176, did not approve of Raymond's policy and immediately put the country on a war footing. The Leper King was very courageous and, despite his disability, enjoyed fighting. Although he had lost the use of his right hand from the start of his reign, he rode to battle with his army and continued to do so until he was too ill to mount, then he was carried into battle in a litter. His chief general was Reynald of Châtillon, who held the two great lordships of Hebron and Transjordan.

Frankish hostility was a severe impediment to Saladin. He had to move his troops between Egypt and Syria by the difficult route through the deep desert because the roads of Transjordan were closed to him; his communications were routinely intercepted; and Frankish military support for the Zengid princes delayed his conquests in north Syria. Prince Reynald even constructed a small fleet which he launched on the Red Sea, disrupting pilgrim traffic between Egypt and the Maghrib and Mecca, thereby calling in question Saladin's effectiveness as protector of the Islamic holy places. In 1177 Saladin mounted an invasion of the Crusader Kingdom from Egypt, but his army, though far superior in number to that of the Franks, was roundly beaten by a force commanded by Prince Reynald and the Leper King at the Battle of Montgisard. Indeed, for as long as Baldwin IV lived, although Saladin attacked the kingdom many times, he did not gain a foot of ground from the Franks.

However, Saladin succeeded in gaining control of the Zengid lands although it took him longer than it would have done had the Franks remained neutral. By

1186 he had secured them all. Raymond of Tripoli, who became regent for the Leper King's little nephew, Baldwin V, when the Leper King died in 1185, made a new truce with Saladin to last for four years.

In 1186 when Baldwin V died, the succession to the kingdom was disputed. The Leper King's elder sister, Sibyl, and her husband, Guy of Lusignan, were crowned and Guy renewed the truce with Saladin but Raymond of Tripoli refused to acknowledge Guy, and made a separate peace with Saladin. With the kingdom so divided, it was clearly a good time for Saladin to launch his attack and in the spring of 1187 he began to assemble a vast army from all over his dominions at Ras al-Mar, near Damascus. He claimed that Reynald of Châtillon had broken the truce by seizing a caravan passing through Transjordan, but had Reynald kept the peace Saladin would almost certainly have found some other pretext for declaring war.

He invaded the kingdom in July and Guy mustered an army some 17,000 strong, which included the traitor Raymond of Tripoli who had belatedly made his peace. This left only small garrisons in the cities and castles of the kingdom, while the treasury was emptied to buy in mercenaries. The two armies were fairly evenly matched in size and met at the Horns of Hattin, a hill overlooking the Sea of Galilee, on 4 July. Although the Franks fought hard, they were not well led. They became cut off from a water supply, essential for the effective deployment of cavalry, and were decisively beaten. Saladin was magnanimous up to a point: the Frankish noble prisoners were well treated, except for Reynald of Châtillon, whom Saladin beheaded with his own hand, and for the Knights Templar and Hospitaller, who were all peremptorily executed on his orders.

It was comparatively easy to subdue the rest of the Crusader States, for the cities and castles were severely undermanned. Jerusalem surrendered on 2 October after a brief siege: the golden cross was pulled down from the Dome of the Rock and Jerusalem became a Muslim city once more. During the next two years Saladin reduced all the Frankish strongholds with the exception of Tyre, Tripoli, Antioch and a few castles.

FIVE

Crusader Kingdom, 1190–1250

When word of the defeat at Hattin reached the West, a new crusade was launched and met with a great response. Henry II of England and his son, Richard Duke of Aquitaine, Philip II Augustus of France, William II of Sicily, and the Emperor Frederick Barbarossa (1152–90), who had gone on the Second Crusade forty years before, all took the cross. This clearly demonstrates how important Jerusalem had become to the people of Western Europe; so many families had members who had fought, and in many cases died, to capture and defend it, while almost everybody knew someone who had been on pilgrimage to the Holy Places since they had come into Catholic hands.

Guy of Lusignan, who had been released by Saladin, led his followers to lay siege to Acre in 1189. Saladin then besieged their camp and the resulting stalemate lasted for about two years. But as a consequence Saladin was forced to keep a substantial part of his army in the field, so that his troops were already war weary when the main crusade finally arrived.

The crusaders' departure from the West was beset with difficulties. War broke out between France and England and although it ended when Henry II died on 6 July 1189, there was further delay for the crowning of Richard I, the Lionheart. Then in November 1189 William II of Sicily died, the succession was disputed and Sicily took no further part in the crusade. The seventy-year-old Frederick Barbarossa, who left the West with a huge army in 1189, was accidentally drowned in a river while crossing Asia Minor; some of his followers returned to the West, others were ambushed by Saladin's troops while negotiating the passes into Syria and only a fraction of the German crusade reached Acre.

The French and English came to Acre by sea in 1191 and their combined forces succeeded in finally breaking the deadlock: Acre surrendered on 12 July. A few weeks later Philip II and most of the French army returned to the West, leaving Richard in command of the crusade. He fought one main battle against Saladin near Arsuf in September 1191, when Saladin's troops were no match for the well-disciplined and heavily mailed English cavalry. This battle proved conclusively to Saladin that he did not have the resources to beat the English field army. Richard stayed in the East for another year but failed to recapture Jerusalem; he did not have enough troops to conduct a successful siege while Saladin's army remained undefeated, but he was not lacking in religious zeal and this failure grieved him.

Against this background Richard and Saladin made peace in September 1192. The Franks received a strip of coastal territory stretching from Jaffa to Tyre, together with those parts of the northern states which Saladin had failed to conquer. A three-year truce was agreed and Frankish pilgrims were guaranteed free access to the Holy Places. Before he left the East, Richard arranged for Guy of Lusignan to become Lord of Cyprus, the former Byzantine island which Richard had annexed on his voyage to the Holy Land. Guy, who was unpopular because of the defeat at Hattin, had lost the support of a substantial part of the baronage after the death of his wife, Queen Sibyl, in 1190, and in 1192 he gave up the crown of Jerusalem in favour of Sibyl's sister, Isabel. The Third Crusade had failed to restore the Latin Kingdom of Jerusalem, but it had assured a continued Frankish presence in the East.

Saladin died on 3 March 1193 and members of his family, the Aiyubids, continued to rule his empire until 1250. But although the Sultans of Egypt were officially the heads of state, their kinsmen who ruled the Syrian provinces were virtually autonomous. This led to frequent civil wars and consequently the Aiyubids did not pose a serious threat to the Crusader States. Moreover, since the economic prosperity of their empire depended in part on trade with the Western powers, they were anxious to avert a new crusade which would involve a trade embargo.

From 1219 onwards the Aiyubids were also preoccupied by the growth of Mongol power to the north of their empire. Between 1219 and 1222 Genghis Khan and the Mongol horde devastated the lands of the Shah of Khwarazm; in 1231 they expanded into Azerbaijan; and in 1243 they subdued the Seljuk sultanate of Iconium. Crusades in the Aiyubid period took place against this background.

In sixty years no fewer than seven crusades were launched to recover Jerusalem. Barbarossa's son, the Emperor Henry VI (1191–7), took the cross in 1195 and the vanguard of his army went to the East in the autumn of 1197 but the unexpected death of the Emperor led to the abandonment of this crusade.

Innocent III (1198–1216) preached a new crusade in 1198. The decision was made to attack Egypt, the centre of Aiyubid power, and the crusade's lay leaders approached Venice to supply transport. They were great noblemen with no financial training and wildly overestimated the size of their army. The Venetians built a fleet to their specifications but, because of the great shortfall of men, the crusade's leaders were only able to meet part of the costs. This inauspicious start led the leaders and the Doge of Venice to view sympathetically the proposal of Prince Alexius, a claimant to the Byzantine throne, that if they would assist him to become emperor, he would maintain the army for a year, pay the Republic of Venice and the crusaders 100,000 marks each, send a force of 10,000 Byzantine troops to Egypt with them, and secure the union of the Byzantine Church with Rome. This plan had attractions for all the participants: Venetian trading privileges in Constantinople would be secure; the papal primacy would be recognized by the Byzantine Church; and the crusade would become financially viable and receive reinforcements.

In the event the outcome was very different, for although Prince Alexius and his elderly father, the deposed Emperor Isaac II, were returned to power by the crusade in July 1203, they were unable to honour their promises, and in April 1204 the crusade attacked Constantinople, sacked it for three days, established a Latin emperor there, and abandoned the projected attack on Egypt. Modern historians tend to express feelings of moral outrage about the sack of Constantinople, but it was viewed very differently at the time. It was the one city of the ancient world which had survived into the central Middle Ages without ever being sacked; its massive fortifications had withstood sieges for almost 800 years and its accumulated treasures were prodigious. The crusade movement had met with no major success since Jerusalem fell in 1099 and the capture of Constantinople was excellent publicity. During the next half century crusading reached the peak of its popularity.

In 1212 a spontaneous outbreak of popular crusading fervour occurred on a scale which had not been seen since the Peasants' Crusade of 1096. This was the Children's Crusade; its participants believed that God would grant a victory to the young and pure in heart which He had denied to their sinful elders. Bands of enthusiastic children converged on the ports of southern Europe, supposing that God would open a path for them through the seas to the Holy Land. But when a miracle failed to occur, the crusade dispersed.

The Fifth Crusade was launched at the Fourth Lateran Council in 1215 and a tax of five per cent was levied on the incomes of the clergy to finance it. This became a regular feature of crusading. The crusade was well supported and attacked Egypt in 1218, capturing the port of Damietta in 1219 after a very long siege. In 1221 when news reached the crusaders of the attack by Genghis Khan and the Mongols on eastern Islam, the papal legate supposed that these were the armies of Prester John, the legendary Christian ruler of the Indies, and that Islam would fall to the combined attack of these Christian forces from East and West. Buoyed up by religious enthusiasm the crusade marched on Cairo in July 1221 just as the Nile was beginning to flood its delta. The crusaders were unable to manoeuvre in the mud and the Aiyubids cut their supply lines and forced them to surrender but they were allowed their freedom in return for withdrawing from Damietta. This papally financed crusade had achieved nothing.

The Emperor Frederick II (1211–50) had taken the cross in 1215 but delayed his departure. In 1225 he married Isabel II, the young Queen of Jerusalem, but still failed to go on crusade. Popes Honorius III (1216–27) and Gregory IX (1227–41) supposed that he was using his crusader status to enlist papal support against his enemies in Lombardy and in 1227 Gregory IX excommunicated him for his failure to fulfil his vow. It then became essential for Frederick's prestige that he should recover Jerusalem without the Pope's support, thereby putting Gregory IX in the wrong in the eyes of the rest of Europe, and in 1228 he took the unusual step of setting out on crusade while excommunicated.

At this time the Sultan of Egypt, al-Kamil (1218–38), was quarrelling with his brothers who ruled Syria. He was not bothered by Frederick's excommunication but regarded him as the lawful King of Jerusalem and the greatest, and also the nearest, Western ruler, for he was both Holy Roman Emperor and King of Sicily. In return for Frederick's neutrality in the Aiyubid civil war, al-Kamil granted him Jerusalem and Bethlehem, with a corridor of land connecting them to the coast, and agreed to a ten-year truce. The Muslims were allowed to keep their holy places in Jerusalem and were guaranteed freedom of worship there but the Islamic world was horrified that Saladin's nephew should gratuitously have surrendered an Islamic holy city to the infidel Franks. Frederick II had achieved what all crusaders set out to do, despite the ban of the Church, but he received little credit for it in the Christian world. This was only partly because of papal hostility, for he made his peace with the Pope in 1231; it was chiefly because of the bad relations that developed between the Emperor and the Jerusalem baronage and plunged the Crusader Kingdom into civil war, preventing the restoration of the Holy City to its former glory.

When the truce was due to expire in 1239, Theobald of Navarre led a new crusade to the Holy Land. Because the Aiyubid princes were locked in a profound and bitter struggle following the death of al-Kamil in 1238, Theobald was able to negotiate an advantageous settlement which restored much of the old kingdom to the west of the Jordan to Frankish rule. He left for France in September 1240, but Richard of Cornwall, nephew of Richard the Lionheart, arrived a month later with a force of English crusaders and the new Sultan, as-Salih Aiyub, confirmed all the concessions which Theobald had gained. This settlement proved very fragile, for when the Sultan summoned Khwarazmian mercenaries to Egypt from north Syria in 1244, the wild horsemen sacked Jerusalem on their way south and massacred the Christian population.

When this news reached the West, Louis IX of France (1226–70) took the cross, and in 1248 set out for Egypt with an army of around 15,000 men. Louis's Crusade looked superficially like a replay of the Fifth Crusade. The French attacked Damietta in June 1249 and the city was immediately abandoned by its timorous garrison. The French army then waited for the Nile floods to subside before marching on Cairo but their advance was blocked by the main Egyptian army outside the city of Mansurah. In the ensuing battle the vanguard, led by Louis's brother, Robert of Artois, was slaughtered, together with almost 300 Templars. This loss of men made victory impossible. Robert of Artois's impetuosity was later blamed for the crusade's defeat but Louis, as commander-in-chief, must share that blame, for instead of withdrawing to Damietta he stayed at Mansurah, trying to turn the defeat into a victory, until the Egyptians cut his supply lines, an epidemic broke out among his malnourished troops, and the French army was forced to surrender. These prisoners, like those taken during the Fifth Crusade, were released in return for the surrender of Damietta and also the payment of a large ransom. Like the Fifth Crusade, Louis IX's Crusade had failed in its attempt to force the rulers of Egypt to restore Jerusalem to Frankish rule.

SIX

Thirteenth-Century Crusader Society

Although the Kingdom of Jerusalem fluctuated in size during the thirteenth century, it never recovered the lands east of the Jordan or the areas around Nablus, Hebron and Gaza. The two northern states, Tripoli and Antioch, were separated from each other by Muslim territory around Latakia (except for a brief period in the 1260s) but because the old line of the Counts of Tripoli had died out, both were ruled out by the Princes of Antioch. In the thirteenth century the princes lived in Tripoli, for Antioch declined in importance after Latakia was restored to Muslim rule in 1188 and the trade of Aleppo was diverted there.

THE KINGDOM OF ACRE

In the southern kingdom the capital was fixed at Acre. The loss of Jerusalem profoundly affected its character. Not only did the court move to Acre, but the Catholic establishment moved there as well. The Latin patriarch and the canons of the Holy Sepulchre, together with the religious communities which served the shrine churches of Jerusalem, all established new churches in exile at Acre, as did Catholic communities from other parts of the kingdom which had passed under Muslim rule. There was no decrease in Western pilgrimage to the Holy Land in the thirteenth century and except in times of war the Muslim authorities placed no obstacles in the way of pilgrims visiting Jerusalem and the other Holy Places in Aiyubid territory. Pope Gregory VIII (1187) had forbidden pilgrims to visit Jerusalem while it was in Muslim hands, so a dispensation had to be obtained by those who wished to go there, but that was no great obstacle. Nevertheless, most pilgrims do not seem to have bothered to make the journey. Although the Muslims were prepared to tolerate them, there were no hostels or other support services for pilgrims of the Latin rite in Jerusalem such as existed in Frankish territory and, in any case, Jerusalem had become once more an alien city, dominated by Islam. So most Western pilgrims confined themselves to visiting the many churches of

Acre and those shrines which remained in Frankish territory throughout much of the thirteenth century, like Nazareth, Mount Tabor, Mount Carmel, the shrine churches of Galilee and Our Lady of Tortosa. Pilgrims may have visited Jerusalem more freely from 1229 to 1244 when it was once again in Catholic control, but the Latin patriarch and his clergy did not return there then, except for a few priests to say Mass at the shrine churches. Thus in the thirteenth century the Crusader Kingdom had lost its spiritual focus: Acre had no Biblical associations and the churches built there by the exiled Jerusalem communities were devotional centres, not shrines built on sites made sacred by the presence of Christ and His Apostles.

THE DECLINE OF ROYAL POWER

The government of the kingdom also changed. The greater part of the crown lands had been lost which reduced royal power considerably and it was further weakened when the crown passed into the female line for three generations. This need not have made it weaker, but Isabel I (1192–1205) had no political capacity, while her daughter, Queen Maria (1205–12), and her granddaughter, Queen Isabel II (1212–28), both died young. Consequently power was exercised either by king consorts, who with one exception came from overseas and had no knowledge of how the kingdom functioned, or by regents chosen from the local baronage. Thus when Frederick II, who married Isabel II in 1225, came to Acre in 1228, there had been no king of Jerusalem for forty years who had grown up in the East and had a power base there.

At their coronation thirteenth-century kings of Jerusalem had to swear, 'I will keep the laws of King Amalric and of King Baldwin his son', that is, the laws in force before 1185. This was, in effect, as risky as signing a blank cheque because the laws were not written down but existed only in the memory of the barons of the High Court. A king consort from Western Europe was therefore at a great disadvantage because his barons alone had the right to define his powers and he was in no position to challenge them from his own knowledge of the past. It is clear from comparing the treatises on the laws of the kingdom written by thirteenth-century baronial lawyers with descriptions of the exercise of royal power contained in contemporary twelfth-century histories that the barons remembered those laws and customs which protected their own rights but conveniently forgot the ones which defined the royal prerogative.

It was this attempt to diminish royal power that brought the barons into conflict with Frederick II, for the Emperor had an unusually high view of the royal office. In the law code which he issued for Sicily he described the king as the 'living law' which God had given to men; this contrasted starkly with the circumscribed view of royal power held by the High Court of Jerusalem. The lawyers had ample opportunity to quibble about Frederick's powers because Isabel II died in 1228, shortly before Frederick went on crusade, having given birth to a son named Conrad. The Emperor thus became in the eyes of the High Court the regent for the child ruler. After Frederick returned to Sicily in 1229 neither he nor Conrad ever went to Acre and the barons were able to interpret the unwritten law, which only they knew, in a way which best suited their own interests.

They began to do so when in 1231 Frederick appointed a new lieutenant, Richard Filangieri, who was not a local baron but a Sicilian nobleman in Frederick's confidence. An influential part of the Jerusalem baronage, led by John of Ibelin, refused to accept the Emperor's right as regent to make this appointment. This led to civil war between the Emperor's supporters and the Ibelins and their supporters, which also involved the baronage of Cyprus, where the Ibelins had considerable influence. It ended in 1233 with the eviction of the imperial troops from Cyprus, where King Henry I came of age and took over the government, and with the division of the Kingdom of Jerusalem, where Richard Filangieri held Tyre and the Holy City while his baronial opponents ruled the rest. In 1242 with Venetian help the Jerusalem barons succeeded in capturing Tyre, thus ending Frederick's rule. When Conrad came of age in 1243 the High Court accepted him as king but refused to accept any lieutenant he appointed unless Conrad first came to Acre and took possession of the kingdom. When he failed to do so they appointed regents to rule in his name, chosen from among his mother's kin living in the East. By that time royal power had become a fiction. Jerusalem was a state ruled by a baronial consortium.

But the barons commanded diminishing sources of power. The authority to appoint the Latin patriarch and his suffragans, which in the twelfth-century had been in the hands of the king, was taken over by the papacy in the thirteenth. This trend was theoretically supposed to be happening all over Western Europe, although in most countries it was modified because of royal opposition, but in the Latin Kingdom of Jerusalem there was no strong ruler to force a compromise on the Roman curia.

THE ITALIAN COMMUNITIES

The Italian communities also became virtually independent of the crown in the thirteenth century. After Saladin's victory the help of the Italian maritime communes had been vital to the survival of the crusader settlements and this had enabled them to renegotiate their treaties. As the ports were recaptured with their help, their property rights were extended and privileges increased – some of them obtained complete immunity for their citizens from royal jurisdiction. Whereas in the twelfth century each Italian colony in each city had been self-governing, in the thirteenth century the home cities appointed officials who had authority over all their citizens in the Crusader States. Thus there was one rector in charge of all the Venetians, two consuls for the Pisans, and three consuls for the Genoese. As a result the Italian communities were able to act as powerful and independent groups. Moreover, the Franks were more dependent on Italian help than ever before; because of their loss of territory they needed to import staple foods from Cyprus and the Greek islands and this necessitated the use of foreign shipping.

The kingdom's trade flourished in the first half of the thirteenth century as the European markets for luxury goods continued to expand. The Pisans, Genoese and Venetians remained the most important traders but they were joined by merchant colonies from other Italian cities like Piacenza, Lucca, Ancona and Florence, and also from Barcelona and the southern French ports. The fact that between 1250 and 1260 more than half the total trade of Genoa was with the Crusader States indicates how important this market was to the mother cities. A strong crown would have profited from this strong economy but the barons of the High Court made no attempt to do so.

THE DEFENCE OF THE CRUSADER STATES

Many noble families had lost their lands as a result of Saladin's conquests but the effects had been softened by Richard I of England's annexation of Cyprus. The Greek landowners there had been dispossessed and the Lusignan kings encouraged noble Franks from the mainland to settle on the island. This did not help the Latin Kingdom because the barons of Cyprus were under no obligation to defend the mainland territories.

The royal army of Jerusalem inevitably declined in size because of the loss of lands and the reduction in the number of crown vassals and the work of defence fell increasingly on the military orders. A new order, that of the Teutonic Knights, had been founded in 1198 by German knights who had gone on Henry VI's crusade. Their rule resembled that of the Knights Templar, but they also had an hospitaller wing. What distinguished them from the older military orders was their ethnic composition, for whereas the Templars and Hospitallers admitted men of all races, the Teutonic Order only recruited from imperial territories. The Teutonic Knights became important during the mastership of Herman of Salza (c. 1210–39), who enjoyed imperial favour, and from 1228 their headquarters was the castle of Montfort near Acre. Although from its early years it assumed commitments in eastern Europe, the order played an important role in the defence of the Christian East, particularly of the Armenian Kingdom of Cilicia.

The Templars and Hospitallers were largely responsible for the defence of the County of Tripoli and the remnant of the old principality of Antioch. Both orders had their headquarters at Acre and their knights and sergeants formed the most professional part of the field army of the Latin Kingdom. The collapse of royal power meant that the orders acted virtually as sovereign bodies. When Louis IX was in the Holy Land he disciplined the Templars for making agreements with Damascus independently of him but normally there was no strong king present to apply checks of that kind.

Although Frankish power was limited and fragmented in the thirteenth century, Frankish territories were preserved because of the continued interest of the Christian West in the recovery of Jerusalem. It was the ambition of all popes and of many kings in the first half of the century to be the instrument whereby the Holy City was once again liberated. The Aiyubids feared to provoke a new crusade by attacking the Frankish settlements and proved remarkably conciliatory to the crusaders who did arrive, even though none of them succeeded in defeating the Egyptian Sultans in the field. Moreover, the maritime republics, whose fleets dominated the Mediterranean, had a vested interest in defending the Crusader States which were the source of a substantial part of their income and where they enjoyed unparalleled privileges and tax concessions.

SEVEN

New Theatres of War

Although the crusade movement had been launched to free Jerusalem it became diversified almost immediately. Pope Urban II discouraged Spanish noblemen from taking the cross because in his view the recovery of Jerusalem and the reconquest of Spain were all part of a single war against a common enemy. In 1118 Pope Calixtus II preached a crusade to recapture Saragossa in Aragon from the Moors and thereafter the Iberian peninsula was regarded as a legitimate theatre of crusading. The Spanish Christians endorsed that view; Alfonso I the Battler, King of Aragon (1104–34), described the Spanish approach to crusading as that of going to Jerusalem by way of Morocco.

The crusade against the pagan Wends which Pope Eugenius III licensed in 1147 as part of the Second Crusade was a new departure. It achieved little in the short term, but it did open up those lands to German colonization and Catholic missions and they had mostly been absorbed into the Western Empire by about 1200. The true importance of the Wendish campaign was that it set a precedent for crusades against pagans.

The precedent for a crusade against Christians was set by Bohemond of Antioch's crusade against the Emperor Alexius I, discussed in Chapter Two.

Nevertheless, for the first hundred years, except in Spain, the crusade was very rarely used for purposes other than the defence of the Holy Land. In the thirteenth century the diversification of crusading theatres of war became more common.

One potential new crusading territory was the Latin Empire of Constantinople. This consisted only of Thrace and parts of mainland Greece, for the Venetians held most of the Greek islands as sovereign rulers. The empire had powerful enemies, notably the Tsars of Bulgaria and the exiled Byzantine Emperors of Nicaea, and it was always short of manpower. Yet although Popes offered crusading privileges to those who were willing to fight in its defence, they met with a general lack of interest until in 1261 the Byzantines recaptured Constantinople and the Latin Empire came to an end. The Venetians retained control of most of the islands and so a Western presence was maintained in the Byzantine world.

CRUSADES AGAINST MOORS

The Christian kings of Spain were aided by the Templars and Hospitallers who founded houses there and the Spanish also founded their own military orders, notably those of Calatrava, Alcantara, Santiago and Avis, to help in the fight against the Moors. Not all the Spanish wars against the Moors were given crusade status by the Popes, any more than were the wars fought by the rulers of the Crusader States against their Muslim neighbours. Nevertheless, crusades were advantageous to the Spanish kings because they gave them more manpower at no extra cost – crusaders gave their services freely.

The final stage of the reconquest began with the victory in the battle at Las Navas de Tolosa in 1212 which was fought by a predominantly Spanish crusading army commanded by Peter II of Aragon. This opened up Andalusia to the Christian advance and made possible the Great Reconquest which, under the leadership of James I the Conqueror of Aragon, and Ferdinand III (better known as San Fernando) of Castile, brought the entire peninsula under Christian rule between 1229 and 1266. Although Moorish emirs continued to reign in

Granada, they were tributary to the crown of Castile. The Spanish success was in no small measure due to the collapse of the Almohad Caliphate in Morocco after 1223 but the fact that these wars had crusade status generated a spirit of religious enthusiasm and commitment among the Christians which aided their victory. Moreover, the generous grants of Church taxes which the papacy made to the Spanish kings enabled them to raise large armies and to keep them in the field for as long as necessary.

Although many Moors fled to Morocco, those who remained under Christian rule enjoyed full religious toleration and little attempt was made to convert them to Catholicism. Indeed, Alfonso X of Castile (1252–84) boasted that he was the king of three religions, that Christians, Muslims and Jews all lived peacefully under his rule.

CRUSADES AGAINST PAGANS

The Baltic Crusade was primarily concerned with the conversion of pagans. In the late twelfth century Russian Orthodox clergy and Catholic missionaries were both at work among the pagans in the Baltic states and a Catholic bishopric was established in

Livonia (modern Latvia). Bishop Albert of Buxhoevden (1199–1229), who was very ambitious, obtained from the Pope the right to preach a perpetual crusade. North German crusaders came to Livonia in most summers and helped to conquer the land which was permanently garrisoned by a new military order, the Knights of the Sword, which Albert founded. Forcible conversion of the Livonians was quite common despite papal disapproval and by the time he died in 1229 Bishop Albert had succeeded in creating a Church state in Livonia, while Estonia had been conquered and evangelized by the Danish crown. The Lithuanians were more powerful and tenacious of their independence than the other Baltic peoples and in 1236 almost completely annihilated the Knights of the Sword. Pope Gregory IX ruled that the remaining knights should be merged with the Teutonic Order.

Since its foundation in 1198 the Teutonic Order had attracted vocations from the high nobility of the Empire and correspondingly lavish endowments. It enjoyed the patronage of the Emperor and the protection of the Pope, but the Latin East did not afford sufficient scope for its activities. In 1225 the Polish Duke of Masovia invited the order to protect his lands against raids by the pagan Prussians, and by the Golden Bull of Rimini in 1226 Frederick II granted the master sovereignty over all conquests made by his order in Prussia. The knights established a base in Culmerland in 1230 and each year, with the support of German crusaders, conquered more Prussian territory and invited Dominican friars to instruct and baptize the subject pagans. In 1237 the order also took over Livonia from the Knights of the Sword.

When the Mongols attacked Russia between 1237 and 1240, the Teutonic Knights in Livonia attempted to profit by attacking the Russians from the west, but were decisively defeated by Alexander Nevsky, Prince of Novgorod, in 1242. When the Mongols swept into eastern Europe in 1241, the Teutonic Knights in Prussia joined with the Poles and Silesians in resisting them and suffered heavy losses at the Battle of Liegnitz. Weakened by these losses, the order could not prevent a revolt in Prussia and this was not suppressed until 1249. Under papal influence moderate terms were imposed on the Prussians. Pagan worship was made illegal but Prussians who became Christians would enjoy free status and keep their lands; they would be eligible to become priests and, if of noble birth, might become Teutonic Knights as well, though any future revolt would be dealt with very severely.

The Mongol invasion had left a power vacuum in western Russia which the Lithuanians moved in to fill. In 1260 they became powerful enough to defeat the Teutonic Knights decisively both in Livonia and Prussia and this triggered a new Prussian revolt which was not finally suppressed until 1295. As a result of this most Prussians were made serfs and their lands were given to German settlers but Lithuania remained pagan and powerful and extremely hostile to the knights, who continued to crusade against it.

CRUSADES AGAINST CHRISTIANS

The thirteenth century also witnessed a great extension in the use of crusades against Christians. The first important campaign of this kind was the Albigensian Crusade preached by Pope Innocent III in 1208 against the Cathar heretics in southern France. Its purpose was not to suppress heresy, for which it was not an appropriate method, but to replace rulers who favoured heretics with Catholic princes who would cooperate with the Church in enforcing the heresy laws. The Albigensian Crusade conferred the same spiritual privileges as a crusade to the Holy Land but participants were only required to perform six weeks' military service in the south of France. It proved hugely popular: vast numbers of men took part from all over Western Europe but particularly from northern France.

During the first phase, which lasted from 1209 to 1215, the lands of southern France between the Rhone and the Garonne were almost all captured with the help of annual crusades coordinated by a north French baron, Simon de Montfort the elder. In 1215 Philip II (1180–1223) of France confirmed him as ruler there but the southern French rebelled against him in 1216 and the crusade was resumed. Simon was killed in the fighting in 1218 and by 1224 his son and successor, Amaury, conceded defeat, withdrew to Paris, and resigned his claims to King Louis VIII (1223–6). The families who had ruled southern France before 1209 resumed power and the Cathars once again practised their faith quite openly. Pope Honorius III persuaded Louis VIII to lead a new crusade in 1226, which was in effect a royal campaign financed by the Church. This led to the imposition by 1229 of royal rule in southern France.

The Albigensian Crusade, initially fought by armies raised by the papacy with minimal reference to the King of France, was a practical demonstration of the temporal power of the Holy See, but that was only possible because royal power in southern France was nominal in 1209. Moreover, the papal crusade ended in failure, and it was only through the intervention of Louis VIII that a settlement favourable to the Church was enforced there.

Both Gregory IX and Innocent IV preached crusades against Frederick II but although they were supported by some of his political opponents in the Empire, they did not succeed in deposing him. The most successful political crusade was that which Pope Clement IV launched against Frederick II's son, King Manfred of Sicily. His kingdom was a papal fief and in theory the Pope had the right to change the succession. Clement IV offered the crown to Charles of Anjou, brother of Louis IX of France, and gave his campaign crusade status. With an army supplied by the French crown and subsidized by clerical taxes, Charles invaded Sicily in 1266, defeated Manfred, and became king. This crusade was a manifestation less of papal power than of French royal power.

THE CONSEQUENCES OF DIVERSIFICATION

The diversification of crusading in the thirteenth century was clearly not detrimental to the interests of the Crusader States since more expeditions were mounted to recover Jerusalem then than ever before. Moreover, although canon lawyers may have argued that all forms of crusading were equally privileged, in the popular mind Jerusalem took precedence over other theatres of war. It was difficult to recruit men for the Albigensian Crusade, for example, in the years 1219 to 1221 when the Fifth Crusade was in Egypt.

Although giving the status of a crusade to wars against the Pope's enemies seems distasteful to twentieth-century sensibilities, there is no evidence that this brought the movement into disrepute at the time as some critics have claimed. Clearly those who went on such campaigns felt no revulsion about crusading against fellow Christians; taking the cross was a voluntary activity, yet thousands of men went on the Albigensian Crusade. Knights enjoyed fighting and the devout among them preferred to fight in a good cause but many were content to let the papacy decide which cause was good.

EIGHT

Crusader Kingdom, 1250–91

At the time of the crusades Muslim armies were not dissimilar from Western armies and consisted of troops supplied by great landowners, bulked out by mercenaries. The only full-time professional soldiers were the Mamluks, who occupied a place rather like that of the military orders in the crusader armies. The arabic word *mamluk* means a chattel but it came to be applied to white boys, chiefly from the Caucasus and the steppes of southern Russia and central Asia, who were bought as slaves and trained as cavalrymen.

The Sultan as-Salih Aiyub (1240–9) had enlisted Mamluks on an unprecedented scale. They were responsible for the defeat of Louis IX's Crusade during the interregnum following the sultan's death and when the young Sultan Turan Shah tried to deprive them of political influence in 1250, they mutinied, killed him and seized power. At first they ruled in the name of an Aiyubid Sultan who was a

young child and their government was challenged
by the Aiyubids who continued to rule in Syria. But
in 1253 the Caliph mediated peace between the two
parties because he feared the Mongol threat, and
the Mamluk emir Aybek was able to proclaim
himself Sultan of Egypt in 1254.

The Caliph's fear of the Mongols was well
founded. Möngke, the new Great Khan of the
Mongols (1251–9), was friendly to Christians and
directed his new offensive against Islam. In 1258 an
army commanded by his brother Hülegü sacked
Baghdad, slaughtering the entire population. The
Mongol princes were pagans, although many of them
had Christian wives and mothers and there were
many Nestorian Christians among the tribes of the
Mongol confederacy. Religious toleration granted to
all subjects on terms of complete parity was part of
the reason for the Mongols' phenomenal success.
This religious situation was known to observers in the
Crusader States but they were uncertain about how
to interpret it. They were undecided whether to treat
the Mongols as a friendly power, well disposed
towards Christians, and, like the Crusaders, an
enemy to Islam, or as ruthless and uncontrollable
pagans bent on world domination who would, if it

suited them, attack Christians as readily as Muslims, as indeed they had shown in their great raid on Europe between 1240 and 1242.

When Hülegü advanced into Syria in 1260 and captured Aleppo, King Hethum of Cilicia and the young Prince Bohemond VI of Antioch did homage to him and received back lands which they had lost since the time of Saladin, including Latakia. The Aiyubid army fled to Egypt and took service with the Mamluks and this enabled Hülegü to withdraw with the major part of his army to Azerbaijan. He is said to have had a force of some 120,000 cavalry and he would certainly have had difficulty in finding adequate fodder in Syria, but he was also concerned to be in a position to return to Mongolia for the election of a new Great Khan, because his brother Möngke had died in 1259.

He left some 15,000 men in Syria, commanded by a Christian general, Kitbuqa, who in March 1260 entered Damascus in triumph, flanked by Bohemond of Antioch and King Hethum of Cilicia. This did indeed look like a Christian victory over the forces of Islam. The Mongols then went on to occupy all the Muslim-held cities of Palestine, including Jerusalem, and completely encircled the Franks of Acre. But the High Court refused

Kitbuqa's demand for submission to the Great Khan, being influenced by the papal legate who distrusted the Mongols because of their savage attacks on Catholic Eastern Europe.

The Mamluks, resolved to prescind an invasion of Egypt, asked the High Court's permission to move their forces through Frankish territory. The High Court agreed to this, and the Mamluk and Mongol armies met at Ain Jalut in Galilee on 3 September 1260: the Mamluks were victorious. This was the first serious defeat that the Mongols had ever suffered on their western campaigns and the Mamluks followed it up by occupying all the interior of Palestine and Syria as far as the Euphrates.

The Franks of Acre have often been criticized for failing to seize the opportunity that the Mongol invasion of Syria presented. Had they joined forces with them, as Bohemond VI had done, the Mamluks could not have chosen so favourable a site for battle and might have been defeated. In such a case the Islamic threat to the survival of the Crusader States would have been completely removed. But the Franks of Acre did not find the prospect of Mongol encirclement any more reassuring than that of Islamic encirclement. The Mongols had behaved with great savagery in Eastern Europe, yet the Franks would have to accept their overlordship. The barons and bishops of Acre, who considered themselves the representatives of a divinely sanctioned Christian world order, could not conceive of being subject to the pagan Great Khan.

Ain Jalut was a decisive battle in a way that few have been. The Mamluks ceased to be regarded as an upstart dynasty of slaves after this victory and were viewed as the saviours of the Islamic world. In 1261 they proclaimed a refugee Abbasid prince as Caliph in Cairo and, as the religious leaders of Sunnite Islam, he and his descendants invested each new Mamluk Sultan. The Sultanate was elective among the Mamluk emirs and military coups were quite frequent but the Egyptian state was very stable because the excellent civil administration, which the Mamluks had inherited from the Aiyubids, was not affected by changes of ruler. The Mamluks developed an immensely powerful army composed of professional soldiers. A proportion of the taxes from designated districts was set aside for the use of the Sultan and of his emirs to be spent on the purchase and training of mamluks. In addition, the taxes of certain other districts were used to support the *Halqa*, the cavalry force of free-born Muslims. This system was gradually extended to new territories which the Mamluks conquered and their armies grew progressively stronger.

The corps of mamluks continued to be recruited from imported white slaves so that its members should be entirely dependent on the Sultan's goodwill. In order to ensure a regular supply of these slaves, the Mamluks allied with the Mongol Khans of the Golden Horde, who ruled south Russia, and white slaves were shipped to Egypt from the ports of the Crimea. The Khans of the Golden Horde were hostile to Hülegü and his descendants, the Il-Khans of Persia, who therefore sought an alliance with the Christian West. Previously they had demanded submission from all foreign rulers but the defeat at Ain Jalut had shaken their self-confidence. In fact this diplomacy proved ineffective, because the slowness of communications between Persia and the West made it impossible to coordinate military strategy, but this was not at first apparent to the Mamluks who were alarmed at the prospect of a joint attack by the Mongols of Persia and a new Western crusade. Under their capable Sultan Baibars (1260–77) they began systematically to attack and capture cities and fortresses in the Crusader States, hoping thereby to deprive future crusades of bases in the Levant.

The Franks were still hopelessly disunited. When in 1268 Frederick II's grandson Conradin was killed, the next in line to the throne of Jerusalem was Hugh III of Cyprus (1267–84), and the High Court offered him the crown. For the first time in almost fifty years the Franks had an adult, resident king, but royal powers had been so eroded in preceding decades that Hugh found the kingdom ungovernable and retired to Cyprus in 1276. The kingdom was further weakened by the rivalry of the Italian maritime republics whose European wars spread to their colonies in the Frankish East. Parts of Acre were laid waste in the 1250s in fighting between the Venetians and Genoese. The war later spread to Tyre and peace was not finally restored until 1277.

Baibars continued his inroads into Frankish territory, his greatest prizes being Nazareth, which he captured in 1263, and Antioch which fell to him in 1268, but he then refrained from further attacks because a new crusade was being prepared in the West. In 1267 Louis IX once again took the cross, as did the Lord Edward and his brother Edmund, the sons of Henry III (1216–72) of England. In 1270 Louis's Crusade sailed to the north African coast to attack Tunis. This has sometimes been seen as a diversion engineered by Louis's brother, Charles of Anjou, King of Sicily, who would have profited from control of this African port but as Jean Richard has argued, Louis himself considered that the Christian cause would be greatly strengthened by capturing Tunis, though he intended this to be a preliminary to a crusade to the Holy Land. But Louis died on 25 August during an epidemic and this led to the abandonment of the whole expedition.

The English contingent, consisting of about 1,000 men, arrived late and went on to the Holy Land in 1271. The Lord Edward made contact with the Il-Khan Abaqa, who sent a force of some 10,000 irregulars into Syria but Edward did not have enough troops to effect a junction with them. While he was at Acre, Tebaldo Visconti, Archdeacon of Liège, who had accompanied him, was elected Pope. Gregory X, as he became, vowed to launch a new crusade and it seems to have been the sultan's awareness of this which led him to offer a ten-year truce to the Franks before Edward left the Holy Land.

The crusade was discussed in 1274 at the Second Council of Lyons, summoned by the new Pope and attended by delegates representing the Il-Khan Abaqa. Support for a crusade was lukewarm. The master of the Templars pointed out how great the logistic problems would be for hosting a crusade of a traditional kind in what remained of the Latin Kingdom and although a new crusade was formally launched, nothing came of it.

The Franks of Jerusalem nevertheless enjoyed a kind of Indian summer. Hugh III's claim to the throne had been contested by his cousin, Mary of Antioch, but in 1277 she sold her claim to Charles of Anjou, King of Sicily. Since Hugh III had effectively abdicated, the High Court recognized Charles as king. He placed a garrison in Acre and the Mamluks kept the peace because they had no wish to antagonize this powerful Western ruler. When he died in 1285 Charles of Anjou was embroiled in a war with Peter III of Aragon who had occupied the island of Sicily but his son, Charles II of Naples, was not interested in the Latin East and withdrew the garrison from Acre. The High Court therefore recognized the new King of Cyprus, Henry II (1285–1324), as King of Jerusalem and he was crowned at Tyre in 1286 amid general rejoicing.

Now that Sicilian protection had been withdrawn the Mamluks felt free to resume their attacks on Frankish territory and, as had happened in the years leading up to Hattin, the Western powers failed to respond to urgent appeals from the Crusader States. The military orders bore the brunt of the fighting but they were no match in numbers for the powerful Mamluk army. Latakia fell in 1287, Tripoli in 1289, and in 1291 the Mamluks laid siege to Acre. The military orders brought in all their available men to defend it; King Henry came there accompanied by knights from Cyprus; and some Western volunteers came too, including a group of Englishmen sent by Edward I (1272–1307) and commanded by Sir Otto de Grandison. Acre fell on 18 May after a six-week siege, although the Templars held out in their headquarters until 8 June. The remaining Frankish strongholds scarcely put up a fight, for they were left with few defenders and knew that no help could reach them in time. Tyre surrendered on 19 May, Sidon on 14 July, Beirut on 31 July, Tortosa on 3 August, and the great Templar fortress of Athlit on 14 August. The Armenian Kingdom of Cilicia remained independent and the military orders held some castles there, but by the end of the summer of 1291 no other Frankish possessions were left in Syria apart from the small island of Ruad, some three miles off the coast of Tortosa, which the Templars held.

NINE

Later Crusades

Although many plans for the recovery of the Holy Land were made in Western Europe in the fifty years after 1291, no major expedition ever took place. Strong practical incentives were lacking. The surviving nobility of the Crusader States retired to Cyprus where most of them already had estates, while the Mamluks systematically destroyed the main ports on the Syrian coast, forcing Western merchants to channel their trade directly through Egypt. In any case, the foundation of the Mongol Empire had opened up important new trading outlets for the West, which were approached through the ports of the Crimea and of Cilicia and were unaffected by the loss of the Crusader Kingdom. After the outbreak of the Hundred Years' War between France and England in 1337 it seemed unrealistic even to plan new crusades, for Germany and Italy were already politically fragmented and there was no major power in the West that was free to lead a new expedition. The only serious attack on Mamluk power in the fourteenth century was the crusade led by King Peter of Cyprus (1359–69), which sacked Alexandria in 1365, but it proved impossible to hold the city for more than a week.

The military orders continued to give institutional expression to crusading ideals. When Acre fell the Templars and Hospitallers set up headquarters in Cyprus, while the Teutonic Knights established theirs in Venice. But in 1307, on the orders of Philip IV of France, Jacques de Molay, the Master of the Templars, was arrested while visiting Paris together with all the French members of his order and accused of idolatry, blasphemy and sodomy. Although there is no evidence that these charges had foundation – the knights only admitted to them when tortured – the order was dissolved by Pope Clement V under pressure from the French crown at the Council of Vienne in 1312. The trial of the Templars gave a powerful incentive to the two surviving international military orders to justify their existence now that the Crusader States had fallen. In 1309 the Hospitallers seized the Greek island of Rhodes and moved their headquarters there. They built a fleet of galleys and for over 200 years made war at sea on Islamic shipping.

In 1309 the Teutonic Order moved its head-quarters to Marienburg in Prussia. It had a papal licence to wage perpetual war against the pagans and used this to launch annual crusades against Lithuania. These expeditions were very popular with the nobility of northern Europe: campaigns were held twice a year, in the summer and in the winter when the order laid on special Christmas festivities for visiting crusaders. The excuse for men who enjoyed fighting to lay waste large parts of Lithuania in the name of Christ was removed in 1386 when the King of Lithuania, Ladislas Jagiello, married Queen Jadwiga of Poland and received Catholic baptism. The two kingdoms were united under Christian rulers and the Teutonic Knights no longer had any justification for crusading against pagans there.

Crusades continued to be fought against the Muslims of north Africa. An international crusade was launched in 1390 against Mahdia in Tunisia, a notorious centre of piracy. It was led by Louis of Clermont, with a French army, and was transported by a Genoese fleet and joined by contingents from

England, Spain and Burgundy. Despite this wide support it achieved nothing. However, in 1415 a Portuguese expedition did capture Ceuta near Tangiers.

The crusading spirit had never died in Spain and it was harnessed by Ferdinand V of Aragon and his wife, Isabella I of Castile, in their war against the Moors of Granada in 1482. The campaign was given full crusade status by Pope Innocent VIII and lasted for ten years. By the time the Catholic Kings finally entered Granada in triumph in 1492 the whole Iberian peninsula had been brought under direct Christian rule. It was Isabella's wish to carry the war into Morocco and this policy was continued after her death in 1504. Key ports were captured along the north African coast and the ambition of Alfonso the Battler to reach Jerusalem by way of Morocco was half achieved in 1510 when the Castilians captured Tripoli in Libya. But because the Spanish were at the same time embarking on their campaigns in the New World, their north African conquests were not consolidated but remained isolated Christian outposts in predominantly Islamic territory. The last Iberian crusade of any consequence was led against Morocco in 1578 by the young King Sebastian of Portugal, with a large army of 1,500 cavalry and 15,000 infantry, which included volunteers from other parts of Catholic Europe. His commanders had no experience of desert warfare and the army was annihilated by the Moroccans at Alcazar in August 1578.

Popes in the later Middle Ages continued to give crusade status to some wars between Christians in Western Europe. These often, though not always, involved the defence of the Papal States and the grant of crusade status was both a sign of the Curia's approval and a means of raising clerical taxes to support the pro-papal side. The Pope's opponents not unnaturally considered such crusades as a cynical manipulation of religion for political ends.

Between 1420 and 1431 five crusades were organized by the Emperor Sigismund against the Taborites, the radical wing of the Bohemian Hussite reform movement. The Taborites' commander, John Žiška, pulverized all these armies, despite their superior numbers and equipment: the Hussite problem, which was in part a religious reform movement but in part a Bohemian nationalist movement, could not be solved by crusading expeditions.

But despite the variety of crusading activities

during this period, the main focus of crusading had changed in the fourteenth century to repelling the growing power of the Ottoman Turks. The Seljuk Turks had been settled in central Asia Minor since the eleventh century. The Ottomans, who took their name from an early sultan called Osman, fled there from the Mongols in the thirteenth century and were given lands in the north-west on the Byzantine frontier. In 1354, when Byzantium had been weakened by civil wars, the Ottomans crossed into Europe; their well-disciplined army bypassed Constantinople, which it lacked the technical skill to besiege, and went on rapidly to conquer Macedonia and much of Thrace. In 1389 it defeated the Serbians at Kosovo and made them tributary, and in 1393 it annexed Bulgaria and reached the Danube.

The Ottomans were now a threat to Catholic Europe and a new crusade was launched, which may justly be considered the last great international crusade. Led by the Count of Nevers, the chivalry of France set out along the Danube valley: 1,000 knights, 1,000 noble squires, 8,000 mercenary infantrymen and twenty-four cartloads of tents and banners made of green velvet embroidered with Cyprus gold thread. They were supported by contingents from Castile and Aragon, Italy, Germany, England, Bohemia, Poland, and Wallachia, and joined up with King Sigismund and the army of Hungary. This huge force did battle with the Ottomans, led by the Sultan Bayezid, outside Nicopolis on the Danube on 25 September 1396 and was completely routed. The combined, but uncoordinated, knighthood of the West had proved no match for the professional cavalry of the Ottomans.

In 1444 a final attempt was made to relieve the beleaguered city of Constantinople, but support came almost entirely from eastern Europe. The young King Ladislas of Hungary and Poland commanded the joint armies of his two kingdoms, accompanied by John Hunyadi, Prince of Transylvania. With a total force of around 25,000 they did battle with the army of the Ottoman Sultan Murad outside Varna on the Black Sea coast on 10 November. Despite being outnumbered, the crusaders almost won. Hunyadi routed the Ottoman cavalry and only the Janissaries, the Sultan's bodyguard, stood firm. Then King Ladislas's knights urged him to lead a charge against the Janissaries so that Hunyadi should not enjoy the sole glory of victory. This proved a grave tactical error, for Ladislas was killed, his head was displayed on a pike, and his demoralized followers fled from the field.

In 1453 the Sultan Mehmed the Conqueror captured Constantinople with the aid of cannon and made it the capital of his empire. He was successfully opposed in his wars of expansion only three times and on each occasion by crusaders. In 1456 he was forced to lift the siege of Belgrade because of the zeal of St John of Capistrano, a Franciscan crusade preacher, who raised an army of some 2,500 Hungarians and led them to the relief of the city. In 1480 the Ottomans captured Otranto in southern Italy and held it for a year until they were driven out by a crusade composed almost entirely of Italian contingents, organized by Pope Sixtus IV (1471–84). Then in 1481 the Sultan's fleet attacked the Knights of St John at Rhodes, but was forced to withdraw.

The Ottoman advance was resumed in 1520 by Suleyman the Magnificent (1520–66) with the capture of Belgrade, followed by that of Rhodes in 1522, where the Knights of St John fought so fiercely that they were allowed to leave with full military honours. Then in 1526 the Ottomans invaded Hungary and defeated the Christian army on the field of Mohács, and in 1529 laid siege to Vienna for the first time.

In 1530 the Emperor Charles V (1519–56) granted Malta to the Knights of St John. They fortified the island and rebuilt their fleet, and since Malta commanded the sea lanes connecting the eastern and western Mediterranean, they proved troublesome to Muslim shipping. In 1565 Suleyman sent an army of some 30,000 men and an armada of 200 ships to Malta. The knights, commanded by their Master, La Valette, put up an extraordinarily courageous fight and succeeded in holding off their attackers from 18 May until 8 September when a Sicilian relief force appeared and the Ottoman fleet withdrew. Although in 1565 Europe was religiously divided as a result of the Protestant Reformation, people throughout the Christian West continued to view crusading activities with favour when they were directed against Islam, and when news of the defeat of the Ottomans at Malta reached England, Queen Elizabeth ordered all the church bells of Protestant London to be rung in thanksgiving.

In 1571, at the end of a long war, the Ottomans captured Cyprus, the last relic of the Crusader States, which since 1489 had been ruled by Venice.

In response Pope Pius V (1565–72) organized a Holy League to defend the Christian Mediterranean and this was joined by the two chief Catholic naval powers, Habsburg Spain and the republic of Venice. Their combined navies, commanded by Charles V's bastard son Don John of Austria, met the Ottoman fleet near Lepanto on the Gulf of Corinth on 7 October 1571 and secured a remarkable victory, sinking 80 vessels and capturing a further 117.

Ottoman expansion seemed virtually at an end in the late sixteenth century and it was therefore a considerable shock to Catholic Europe when in 1683 the Ottomans invaded Austria and laid siege to Vienna. Although they were forced to withdraw, this act of aggression led Pope Innocent XI to found a new Holy League in 1684 which was joined by the Emperor Leopold I, the King of Poland and the Venetian republic. The participants were granted crusading tithes on clerical incomes and the war which followed was undoubtedly understood in religious terms by the Christian powers, though it is not clear whether any of them formally took crusade vows. It led to the permanent expulsion of the Ottomans from almost the whole of Hungary and Transylvania, and to the temporary conquest by the

Venetians of most of the Peloponnese between 1685 and 1715. These, and the wars waged against the Ottomans by Leopold I's successor, Charles VI (1711–40), were the last wars fought by Catholic powers against Islam which were characterized by the same religious fervour as the medieval crusades.

The Knights of St John continued to rule Malta and to protect their own subjects and much Christian shipping in the western Mediterranean from the attacks of the Barbary Corsairs until Napoleon captured the island in 1798. The Knights of St John and the Teutonic Order, both founded to defend the Holy Land, still exist as religious orders of the Catholic Church but their work is now entirely liturgical and philanthropic.

Conclusion

Although some modern writers claim that the crusades did permanent damage to relations between Christians and Muslims, there is little evidence of this in contemporary sources. Christians and Muslims in the Middle Ages were not very interested in the abstract principles underlying each others' faith; each was aware of the other as a community whose members were bound together by a religious faith which differed from their own. Muslims, who had since the seventh century waged the *jihad* against the Christian powers in the Mediterranean, were not aghast when Christians conducted their own holy wars in return. War breeds atrocities; both sides committed them and this did not help to further friendly relations between them. However, this was not a consequence of the crusades but of a war which began centuries before them and lasted long after they had ended.

The primary purpose of the crusades was to liberate Jerusalem. This was achieved and the city remained in Western hands for eighty-eight years. During that time the Franks turned it into a Catholic city, full of shrine churches built to Western designs and served by religious communities who celebrated the liturgy each day in the Latin rite. The many pilgrims who travelled there each year from the West were able to see the events of the Gospels liturgically reenacted in a familiar form in the places where Christ had lived among men. This led to the growth among Western Christians of a deep devotion to the humanity of Christ, which found its first widespread popular expression in the preaching of St Francis of Assisi and his followers in the early thirteenth century, and which has remained central to all forms of Western Christian piety ever since. That is the most lasting bequest of the crusades to the Western world.

Not all the consequences of the crusaders' presence in the Levant were equally benign. Initially they fulfilled Urban II's declared aim and helped their Eastern brethren in Byzantium by enabling them to recover western Asia Minor. It was the armies of the First Crusade who defeated the Turkish Sultan there and who did not attempt in any way to profit from this victory, but left the Byzantines to occupy the rich coastal provinces and confine the Turks to the barren interior plateau. Yet it was also a crusade which sacked Constantinople in 1204 and fatally weakened Byzantium which had protected Christian Europe against Islamic invasions for centuries. Although the Byzantines recovered the capital in 1261 they could never reconstitute the empire which the Fourth Crusade and its Venetian allies had fragmented, and that undoubtedly facilitated the Ottoman conquest of the Balkans in the late Middle Ages.

It is difficult to estimate the effect of the crusades on the Iberian peninsula. The Moors were driven out and Spain and Portugal became integral parts of Western Christendom again, not, as most of the peninsula had been in the year 1000, an annexe of the Islamic Maghrib. Yet the wars of reconquest began long before the crusades and most of them were fought by Spanish kings without much outside help. It is therefore arguable that the Christian reconquest would have happened even if Spain had never become a theatre of crusading activity, but such a judgment needs qualifying. The additional manpower and expertise which crusader volunteers brought to some of the early twelfth-century campaigns was undoubtedly critical; as were the crusade taxes which thirteenth-century popes allowed the kings to levy on the Spanish Church, enabling them to support armies large enough to follow through their victories. But most important of all was the unity of purpose which the crusading ethic gave to the politically fragmented Spanish Christians.

Arguably the crusading movement produced its most long lasting effect in the eastern Baltic where the process of Russian settlement and evangelization was halted and the pagans were drawn into the religious and cultural orbit of Western Europe, with the result that Russia was for centuries excluded from the Baltic ports.

Viewed as a whole the crusading movement achieved its objective of making warfare respectable in Western Christian society. Whereas eleventh-century fighting men had experienced a conflict between their faith and their way of life, the crusades helped to shape the concept of the Christian knight who devoted his life to the protection of the weak and the defence of God and His Church. By the thirteenth century the knight Galahad could be used as a literary symbol of Christian perfection. Conversely, warfare between Christians became acceptable to the Church and has remained so, whereas in the generation before the First Crusade the Normans who fought at Hastings had been required to do penance for killing fellow Catholics.

The effect of the crusade on the papacy was ambivalent. When the popes preached crusades against Islam they were able to give the peoples of Catholic Europe a unity of purpose which they would otherwise have lacked and this increased papal prestige. Conversely, the fact that the popes had, through the crusades, demonstrated their capacity to summon large armies and to raise large sums of money by taxing the clergy did not benefit them in the long term because secular rulers devised ways of exploiting those powers for their own ends and the papacy was manipulated by them.

It is easy to emphasize the negative results of crusading. Large numbers of people died in pursuit of an ideal and many non-combatants were killed; that is an inevitable consequence of prolonged warfare. But I have tried to show that the crusade movement had a more positive effect on the way in which Western society developed. Certainly on a popular level crusading has retained a positive image: throughout the whole of Western Europe today, Protestant as well as Catholic, the term crusade is invariably used of movements and causes which enjoy public esteem.

Glossary

Abbasids The dynasty of Caliphs (q.v.) of Baghdad who ruled from 750 until the Mongol sack of 1258.

Aiyubids The family of Saladin (called from his father, Aiyub), who ruled in Egypt from 1171 to 1250.

Albigensians A name sometimes given to southern French Cathars (q.v.), who had their first bishopric at Albi.

Almohads The dynasty which ruled in Morocco from 1147 to 1269, and for part of that time controlled Muslim Spain.

Anatolia Another name for Asia Minor (i.e. the Asiatic provinces of modern Turkey).

Armenian Church By the time of the Crusades the Armenian Church was a completely independent body, no longer in communion with the Byzantine Orthodox Church.

Barbary Corsairs Muslim pirates operating out of the north African ports, especially Algiers, from the sixteenth to the early nineteenth centuries.

Byzantine Empire The name given to the eastern provinces of the Roman Empire ruled in the Middle Ages from Constantinople (in Greek, Byzantium). In 1050 the Empire stretched from the Danube to north Syria but was gradually diminished until the Ottoman conquest in 1453.

Caliph The successor of the Prophet Muhammad as head of the Islamic community. Religious divisions sometimes led to the appointment of rival Caliphs, and Caliphs often delegated their temporal authority to Islamic princes.

101

Cathars Christian dualist heretics who taught the existence of two gods and who flourished in southern France and Lombardy in the period 1140 to 1320.

Cilicia From 1198 to 1375 an independent Armenian kingdom in south-east Asia Minor.

Fatimids The dynasty of Shi'ite (q.v.) Caliphs who ruled in Cairo from 969 until Saladin removed them from power in 1171.

Franks The name, used by themselves and also by the Muslims, for Western European settlers in the Levant.

Holy Roman Empire Broadly speaking the territories of Germany, Switzerland and northern Italy ruled by an elected emperor whom the Pope crowned.

Hussites Followers of the Bohemian reformer, John Hus (d. 1415).

Jacobites Members of the independent church founded in the sixth century by Jacob Baradaeus in Syria and Mesopotamia, now normally called the Syrian Orthodox Church.

Jihad The holy war against unbelievers enjoined by the Prophet Muhammad on his followers.

Khwarazm The area around the mouth of the Oxus river in central Asia whose rulers styled themselves shahs. After the Mongols destroyed their state in 1231 their army became mercenaries in the service of the Aiyubid sultans.

Maghrib Western Islamic lands: north Africa and Moorish Spain.

Maronites The Christians of Mount Lebanon who formed an independent church at the time of the crusades and entered into union with Rome after 1181.

Moors The name usually given to the Muslims of Spain.

Nestorians The principal Christian church in Asia in the Middle Ages, which numbered among its followers the Kerait and Naiman peoples of the Mongol confederacy.

Ottomans A Turkish people who took their name from an early Sultan called Osman and founded the Ottoman Empire which lasted until 1922.

Papal legate The representative of the Pope for a particular mission (e.g. on a crusade).

Prester John A legendary Christian king believed in the twelfth and thirteenth centuries to rule in 'the three Indies' which lay beyond the Islamic lands.

Seljuks Seljuk, an early leader, gave his name to this Turkish people who dominated the lands of the Caliph of Baghdad at the time of the First Crusade. One branch of the Seljuks conquered Byzantine Asia Minor and founded the Sultanate of Iconium.

Shi'ites One of the main religious divisions in the Islamic world. The Shi'ites regard the Prophet's son-in-law Ali, the third caliph, and his descendants as the lawful Imams, divinely guaranteed interpreters of the Islamic revelation and rightful heads of the Islamic community.

Sunnites The other main religious division in the Islamic world, who believe that the interpretation of the Prophet's revelation is vested in the whole community of the faithful.

Thrace The area around Constantinople, roughly corresponding to the part of modern Turkey west of the Bosphorus.

Turks People who speak Turkish. This is *not* a general word meaning Muslims.

Vizier The chief minister of a medieval Islamic ruler.

Wends The Slav peoples who lived in north Germany between the Elbe and the Oder before this region was conquered and settled by the Germans in the twelfth century.

Zengids The descendants of Zengi, ruler of Mosul and Aleppo (d. 1146).

Further Reading

GENERAL WORKS

Finucane, R.C. *Soldiers of the Faith. Crusaders and Moslems at War* (London, Dent, 1983), a perceptive attempt to write crusading history from the point of view of the participants.

Holt, P.M. *The Age of the Crusades. The Near East from the Eleventh Century to 1517* (London, Longman Group Ltd, 1986), examines the Islamic context in which the crusades took place.

Mayer, H.E. *The Crusades*, tr. J. Gillingham (2nd edn, Oxford, Oxford University Press, 1988), is an excellent and succinct account of crusades to the East.

Riley-Smith, J. (ed.) *The Atlas of the Crusades* (London, Swanston Publishing Ltd, 1990), maps with commentaries produced by a team of experts.

Riley-Smith, J. (ed.) *The Oxford Illustrated History of the Crusades* (Oxford, Oxford University Press, 1995), an excellent collection of monographs on crusading history, including that of the later crusades.

Riley-Smith, J.R.S. *The Crusades. A Short History* (London, The Athlone Press, 1987), deals with all crusading theatres of war.

Runciman, S. *A History of the Crusades*, 3 vols (Cambridge, Cambridge University Press, 1951–4), is the classic work on the history of crusades to the East.

SOURCES IN TRANSLATION

Arab Historians of the Crusades, tr. F. Gabrielli, (tr. from Italian by E.J. Costello (London, Routledge and Kegan Paul, 1969).

Chronicles of the Crusades. Eyewitness accounts of the wars between Christianity and Islam, ed. E. Hallam (Godalming, CLB International, 1989).

Documents on the Later Crusades, ed. and tr. N.J. Housley (London, 1996).

DETAILED STUDIES

Barber, M. *The New Knighthood. A History of the Order of the Temple* (Cambridge, Cambridge University Press, 1994).

Folda, J. *The Art of the Crusaders in the Holy Land, 1098–1187* (Cambridge, Cambridge University Press, 1995), a beautifully illustrated account of the cultural history of the Crusader Kingdom.

Forey, A. *The Military Orders* (London, Macmillan Education Ltd, 1992), deals with all the crusading orders in the Middle Ages.

France, J. *Victory in the East. A Military History of the First Crusade* (Cambridge, Cambridge University Press, 1994).

Hamilton, B. *The Latin Church in the Crusader States* (London, Variorum Publications Ltd, 1980).

Housley, N. *The Later Crusades. From Lyons to Alcazar, 1274–1580* (Oxford, Oxford University Press, 1992), provides an excellent coverage of all crusading theatres of war.

Kennedy, H. *Crusader Castles* (Cambridge, Cambridge University Press, 1994), deals with castles in the Crusader States.

Kennedy, H. *Muslim Spain and Portugal* (London, Addison Wesley Longman Ltd, 1996), a history of Moorish Spain and its loss.

Lock, P.W. *The Franks in the Aegean, 1204–1500* (London, Longman, 1995), deals with the Latin Empire of Constantinople and the long-term effects of the Fourth Crusade.

Mackay, A., *Spain in the Middle Ages. From Frontier to Empire, 1000–1500* (London, Macmillan Press Ltd, 1977), an analytical account of the Spanish reconquest.

Macquarrie, A.D. *Scotland and the Crusades* (Edinburgh, 1985), an excellent account of a neglected aspect of crusading.

Morgan, D. *The Mongols* (Oxford, Blackwell, 1986), a learned and entertaining account of Mongol history.

Powell, J.M. (ed.) *Muslims under Latin Rule, 1100–1300* (Princeton, Princeton University Press, 1990), a comparative study of Spain, Sicily and the Crusader States.

Prawer, J. *The History of the Jews in the Latin Kindom of Jerusalem* (Oxford, Clarendon Press, 1988).

Prawer, J. *The Latin Kingdom of Jerusalem. European Colonialism in the Middle Ages* (London, Weidenfeld and Nicolson, 1972), an account of the society of the Crusader Kingdom.

Sumption, J. *The Albigensian Crusade* (London, Faber and Faber, 1978), an excellent military history of the crusade, though less good on the Cathar heresy.

Thoreau, P. *The Lion of Egypt. Sultan Baybars I and the Near East in the Thirteenth Century*, tr. P.M. Holt (London, Longman, 1987), an account of the Mamluk impact on the Crusader States.

Tyerman, C. *England and the Crusades, 1095–1588* (Chicago and London, University of Chicago Press, 1988), the only modern treatment of the English contribution to the crusades.

Urban, W. *The Baltic Crusade* (De Kalb, Ill., 1975), and *The Prussian Crusade* (Washington D.C., 1980), give a full account of the crusade against pagans in the eastern Baltic.

Index